Lectionary Worship Aids

Series V, Cycle A

Dallas A. Brauninger

CSS Publishing Company, Inc., Lima, Ohio

LECTIONARY WORSHIP AIDS, SERIES V, CYCLE A

Copyright © 1998 by
CSS Publishing Company, Inc.
Lima, Ohio

The original purchaser may photocopy material in this publication for use as it was intended (i.e. worship material for worship use; educational material for classroom use; dramatic material for staging or production). No additional permission is required from the publisher for such copying by the original purchaser only. Inquiries should be addressed to: Permissions, CSS Publishing Company, Inc., P.O. Box 4503, Lima, Ohio 45802-4503.

Library of Congress Cataloging-in-Publication Data

Brauninger, Dallas A., 1943-
  Lectionary worship aids. Series V / Dallas Brauninger.
     p.   cm.
  Includes bibliographical references and index.
  Contents: [1] Cycle A.
  ISBN 0-7880-1209-6 (cycle A : alk. paper)
  1. Worship programs. 2. Church year. 3. Common lectionary (1992) I. Title.
BV198.B66   1998
264—dc21   98-2527
                                                                 CIP

This book is available in the following formats, listed by ISBN:
     0-7880-1209-6   Book
     0-7880-1210-X   IBM
     0-7880-1211-8   MAC
     0-7880-1212-6   Sermon Prep

PRINTED IN U.S.A.

To Cheryl

Table Of Contents

Preface

Hymns engage persons in worship ... The beginning hymn catches our attention and binds us together ... Creatively presented, a hymn can charm its way into your congregation. Occasionally, provide the tonic of an old-fashioned, memorized hymn, a comfort whose words and automatic tune need not trouble aging eyes ... Congregations accept new words more readily than they learn new tunes. If yours is shy about trying new tunes, first introduce words set to an appropriate, familiar tune. Find compatible tunes for the meter and spirit of the words by using the tune and metrical indices in your hymnal.

These excerpts from a recent series on hymns in *Emphasis: A Preaching Journal For The Parish Pastor*[1] set the tone for the selection of hymns in this worship resource.

The hymns of the church potentially bind our churches together during these times of new clergy sharings among denominations. Merging of congregations promises to bring together a unique mix of clergy and laity. Pastors bring their own repertoires of hymns to a congregation. The greater variety of people opens the way for new sharings. New hymnals expand the possibilities of the sung word in a new century. New tunes refresh well-known words, new words renew well-known tunes.

The revival of certain classical hymns helps diminish denominational homesickness of parishioners. Can a Methodist thrive long without singing "Here I Am, Lord," an Episcopalian without "Come [Down][Forth], O Love Divine," a Presbyterian without "Amazing Grace," or a member of the United Church of Christ without "Christian, Rise And Act Thy Creed"? Might many of our denominations one day share one hymnal?

Hymns for each worship service are coded from 01A through 68A for easy location in the index of hymns at the end of this volume. While this list includes several representative denominational hymnals and two collections by contemporary hymn writers, it is not exhaustive.

Hymn selection for the three cycles of this series offers as much information as lectionary recommendation. The writer means to

7

integrate the rich heritage of classical hymn texts and tunes spanning the denominations with the introduction of less frequently sung tunes and hymns new to the decade.

In several instances where a hymn may not be readily available, the bold-type, upper case "OR" indicates an alternative hymn selection. The lower case "or" marks an optional tune. Such options lend themselves as "teaching hymns" sung often during a month or season.

Several footnoted suggestions submit additional uses of hymns. For example, a verse of "Come, [O][Thou] Long-Expected Jesus" used as a closing congregational response at the extinguishing of the candles throughout Advent ties together the season. Other connecting hymns periodically serve as congregational calls to worship and prayer responses. Some selections offer a congregation/choir duet of a well-known tune with the familiar words and a refreshed text. The antiphonal singing of a hymn completes other services. Certain times of the year, the writer suggests congregational choice of hymns.

As another goal of this series of lectionary worship aids, the writer has reached toward a conversational, familiar manner of prayer in the calls to worship, collects, and prayers of confessions. It is hoped that they minimize the religious cliché and will assist worship leaders in drawing today's worshipers toward closer union with each other and with God.

---

1. See Brauninger's "Hymns In The Worship Environment," The Worship Environment Column in *Emphasis: A Preaching Journal For The Parish Pastor*, Volume 26, Numbers 2-6 (July-August, 1996 — May-June, 1997).

First Sunday In Advent

First Lesson: Isaiah 2:1-5
Theme: With Joy

Call To Worship
Leader: With joy you will draw water from the wells of salvation.
People: God is our strength and our might.
Leader: Surely God is our salvation.
All: We will trust and be unafraid.

Collect
You do make a difference in our lives, O God. Our enthusiasm for meeting each day grows stronger as we anticipate your saving action on this earth. In the name of the living God. Amen.

Prayer Of Confession
We all need your comfort, O Gracious and Forgiving God. We need peace from inner and outer assault. We yearn, O God, for wholeness. Free us from pain of burden and distress. Be strength for us. Be the strongest force in our lives so that we will trust and not be afraid. Amen.

01A Hymns[1]
"Creator Of The Stars Of Night" Tune: CONDITOR
"We Yearn, O [Christ][God], For Wholeness" Tune: PASSION CHO-
    RALE
"Comfort, Comfort [O][These][Ye] My People" Tune: PSALM 42

First Sunday In Advent

Second Lesson: Romans 13:11-14
Theme: Choose Light

Call To Worship

Leader: Advent has come.
People: Advent is here.
Leader: Lay aside darkness.
People: We call out for hope.
Leader: Lay aside hiding among shadows.
People: We look for the light.
All: Light will come.

Collect

Nudging God, let us dare to surrender to the coming light of Jesus' birth. Let us give in to your nudge to hope. Let us gather as people who choose to follow your light. Amen.

Prayer Of Confession

Listening God, you hear us even when we shrink within private darkness. We choose the dark, letting its works crowd out the strength of light. We cloak ourselves with the shadows of the dark. We confess that the darkness is comfortable. We let it obscure what is true about us, then wonder why others do not really know us. Forgive us for choosing the easy way. Forgive our forgetting that you are with us in the dark. Amen.

01A Hymns[1]

"[O][Oh] Come, O Come, Emmanuel" Tune: VENI EMMANUEL
"Almighty God, Give Us The Grace" Tune: TALLIS' CANON
"Watchman [Watcher], Tell Us Of The Night" Tune: ABERY-STWYTH

First Sunday In Advent

Gospel: Matthew 24:36-44
Theme: Keep Awake

Call To Worship

Leader: Keep awake. Keep from spiritual snoozing through winter's gloom. Push away the desert of lethargy.
People: Now is the time to be attentive to matters of the heart. Advent has begun.
Leader: Keep awake. Don't let boredom be your attitude of choice. Rouse your interest in important matters.
People: Now is the time to sort the vital from the trivial. Advent has begun.
Leader: Keep awake. Be ready for the action of God. Pay attention to what is coming.
People: Now is time to make ready for hope. Advent has begun.

Collect

Quiet the noise within us, O God, the anxious prattle that muffles hope, so we might be alert for moments to glimpse the holy within and live beyond the earthly-minded. Amen.

Prayer Of Confession

When first thoughts about Advent and Christmas months slipped in months ago, somehow, God, the swell of hope was more spontaneous than now when we are already caught in the rush. Sustain us these days that we might stay alert to the right matters, those of the heart. For the sake of Jesus. Amen.

01A Hymns[1]

"Keep Awake, Be Always Ready" or "Wake, Awake, For Night Is Flying" Tune: WACHET AUF
"O Splendor Of God's Glory Bright" Tune: PUER NOBIS NASCITUR, SPLENDOR PATERNAE, or WAREHAM
"Let All Mortal Flesh Keep Silence" Tune: PICARDY

---

1. 01A is the code number for locating suggested hymns for today in various denominational hymnals. During the Sundays of Advent, use verse one of "Come, [O][Thou] Long-Expected Jesus" as a benediction response.

Second Sunday In Advent

First Lesson: Isaiah 11:1-10
Theme: From Jesse's Stump

Call To Worship

Leader: The spirit of God shall rest on him,
People: This little child who will lead us.
Leader: The spirit of wisdom and understanding shall rest on him,
People: This little child who will lead us.
Leader: The spirit of counsel,
People: This little child.
Leader: The spirit of knowledge and the fear of God.
People: His name is Jesus.

Collect

From the time of his birth, O Holy Creator, nations and persons have been curious about your child. Increase our curiosity this Advent season so we also might be led by him with roots from the beginning of time. Amen.

Prayer Of Confession

Could it be, O God, that we too might make decisions equitable for all people, decisions based not on superficial observance and overhearing but on the fairness and justice of high moral standards — because of this little child's showing us the way? We pray with expectation. Amen.

02A Hymns

"Lo, How A Rose [E'er Blooming][Is Growing]" Tune: ES IST EIN' ROS'
"A World Of Love And Peace" Tune: PACEM
"Almighty God, Give Us The Grace" Tune: TALLIS' CANON

Second Sunday In Advent

Second Lesson: Romans 15:4-13
Theme: Embrace Hope

Call To Worship

Leader: Lay aside discouragement, take on hope.
People: Come, Quiet One, slip into our hearts.
Leader: Lay aside resignation, hug tenacity.
People: Come, Holy Child, stir our caring.
Leader: Lay aside unfaithful attitudes, be steadfast.
All: We welcome your coming.

Collect

God of Hope, let us know the peace of believing. Let us hear the truths of the Bible as more than empty, old words. Let us come as your people wanting again to be faithful, beginning anew to practice being honorable. Amen.

Prayer Of Confession

Christmas again, so what? Christmas again, so we give gifts from duty? Christmas again, so we overeat, over-everything? Christmas again, so we feign having the spirit? Help us, Steadfast God, to listen to the story with the first-time hearing of children. Amen.

02A Hymns

"Come, [O][Thou] Long-Expected Jesus" Tune: STUTTGART
"O How Shall I Receive You" Tune: ST. THEODULPH
"Hark The Herald Angels Sing" Tune: MENDELSSOHN

Second Sunday In Advent

Gospel: Matthew 3:1-12
Theme: A Straight Path

Call To Worship

Leader: From the beginning, nothing about Jesus is devious. The paths that John the Baptist prepares for Jesus are straight.

People: We are weary from circling aimlessly through a densely wooded life filled with too many choices and few good purposes. We are ready to follow straight paths.

Leader: Let us untie the knots and straighten the tangles from our lives so our path to the manger follows a straight, uninterrupted course.

People: Through our wanderings, we have created crooked paths of uncertainty, indecision, and doubt.

All: Come, let us clear the way for hope.

Collect

The infant we expect will mature to walk down many paths as a trailblazer for you, O God. As he clears paths to set us free from our fears and sins, let us make a path from our hearts to receive him. Amen.

Prayer Of Confession

Inspire us to turn away from generating chaos. Still us from cluttering the path with debris. Give strength to our turning toward you as we await the holy birth. Amen.

02A Hymns

"Come, [O][Thou] Long-Expected Jesus" Tune: STUTTGART
"The Baptist Shouts On Jordan's Shore" Tune: WINCHESTER NEW
"To Shepherds As They Watched By Night" or "While Shepherds Watched Their Flocks" Tune: WINCHESTER OLD

Third Sunday In Advent

First Lesson: Isaiah 35:1-10
Theme: Set Aside Sighing

Call To Worship

Leader: Be strong, walk the walk of God's way.
People: For here is our God.
Leader: Lay aside your lameness of soul, leap into faith.
People: Here comes strength for our souls.
Leader: Let go of your sigh, give words to your song.
All: For here is our God, here comes strength for our souls.

Collect

We come, O God, to catch a note of the angel's song. We come to hear about peace on earth. We come to mete out goodwill to all. We gather here to sing the great news of joy. Amen.

Prayer Of Confession

Accepting God, we come filled with sorrows we share with no one else. Help us give words to our sighing. Listen to our fears. Hear our disappointments. Attend to the lameness within our souls. Understand the silence we muffle with words. Accept what is bleak about us so we might know strength. Amen.

03A Hymns

"It Came Upon A Midnight Clear" Tune: CAROL
"There's A Song In The Air" Tune: CHRISTMAS SONG
"In The Bleak Midwinter" Tune: CRANHAM

Third Sunday In Advent

Second Lesson: James 5:7-10
Theme: Be Patient

Call To Worship

Leader: Be as patient for the coming of God as the farmer waits for the precious crop from the earth.

People: Break forth, O beautiful light.

Leader: Be patient while waiting for the early rains that will bring up the plants.

People: Break forth, O beautiful light.

Leader: Be patient while enduring too much moisture at the wrong time or drought or extreme heat.

People: Break forth, O beautiful light.

Leader: Be patient while hoping for harvest before the hail.

All: Break forth, O beautiful light.

Collect

Waiting is hard, O God. So many hours in our life are spent in anxious waiting, impatient waiting, and urgent waiting. Strengthen our hearts to endure. Amen.

Prayer Of Confession

Teach us to be resolute in our waiting, O God, to hold our tongue from grumbling, to avoid taking our impatience out on those around us. Teach us the peace of waiting when that which we await means life for us. Amen.

03A Hymns

"Break Forth, O Beauteous Heavenly Light" Tune: ERMUNTRE DICH

"All Earth Is Waiting" Tune: SEDONA

"From Heaven Above To Earth I Come" Tune: VOM HIMMEL HOCH

Third Sunday In Advent

Gospel: Matthew 11:2-11
Theme: Are You The One?

Call To Worship

Leader: Are you the one who will insist we remove poverty?

People: Are you the one who will lead us away from misuse of drugs, alcohol, and food?

Leader: Are you the one who will steer us toward treating all people as worthy of respect?

People: Are you the one who will persuade us to return to the education of our children?

Leader: Are you the one who will motivate us to work on chronic diseases until we solve their mysteries?

People: Are you the one who will show us how to love ourselves and others?

All: Are you the one?

Collect

You are the one, O Awaited Messiah, we expect to work miracles in this world. Let us respond to your coming by doing our part. For your sake. Amen.

Prayer Of Confession

Hope, joy, love, peace — so short are these words of Christmas. So far-reaching are their consequences. Let us be the ones, O God, to keep them alive. Amen.

03A Hymns

"The First Nowell" Tune: THE FIRST NOWELL
"Christ, Whose Glory Fills The Skies" Tune: RATISBON
"We Hail You God's Anointed" Tune: ELLACOMBE

Fourth Sunday In Advent

First Lesson: Isaiah 7:10-16
Theme: A Sign

Call To Worship

Leader: Do you suppose that God's infant coming is to remind us that our beginning as Christians is like that of children who at first do not know how to refuse the evil and choose the good?

People: Do you suppose God is telling us that we need growing time with guidance and nurture rather than expecting immediately to be mature in our faith?

Collect

So great is your love for us, O Thou who sees beyond what we know and reaches beyond our understanding. You prepare us for your coming by sending the angels' songs and the shepherds' rejoicing to announce amid all the bleakness that this, indeed, is something good. Therefore, we rejoice. Amen.

Prayer Of Confession

We, who need signs from you, O God, so that we might stand firm in our faith, wait anew for the birth. We come each Advent as new persons, changed by the events of the past year and ever-needy of signs to renew our faith. Amen.

04A Hymns

"It Came Upon The Midnight Clear" Tune: CAROL
"[O][Oh] Come, O Come, Emmanuel" Tune: VENI EMMANUEL
"Angels We Have Heard On High" Tune: GLORIA

Fourth Sunday In Advent

Second Lesson: Romans 1:1-7
Theme: Grace And Peace

Call To Worship

By addressing Gentiles and Romans, the apostle Paul stretches the realm of Christianity. If we allow him also to greet us, then we, too, will hear the call to announce the good news by the way we live and by the things we do in our communities. So I say his words to you today: Grace to you and peace from God our Parent and Jesus Christ our Savior.

Collect

Christians not only choose to belong to Jesus Christ, we are called by you, O God, to belong to him. In these days of celebrating the birth of God on earth, bring us to a fuller understanding of what it means to belong to Christ. Amen.

Prayer Of Confession

Because we are yours, O God, your first concern is to convey grace and peace to us. How often we greet others — perhaps our only meeting — with a careless "How are you?" that says nothing. Remind us in this holy season to bring God's peace and grace when greeting others — because we are yours. Amen.

04A Hymns

"[O][Oh] Come, All Ye Faithful" Tune: ADESTE FIDELES
"Away In a Manger" Tune: AWAY IN A MANGER
"Joy To The World" Tune: ANTIOCH

Fourth Sunday In Advent

Gospel: Matthew 1:18-25
Theme: Look For Signs

Call To Worship

Leader: Lay aside fear, pick up your courage.
People: God is coming soon.
Leader: Stop your hesitating, start believing.
People: God is coming soon.
All: **We look for signs of God-with-us, Emmanuel. We have come to put on faith. God is coming soon.**

Collect

We come as your people, dear God, with the quiet faith of expectation. We come as earthly citizens filled with imperfections and with being less than we know we can be. We come, nevertheless, because you have loved us so dearly that you are coming to us. Amen.

Prayer Of Confession

When something seems beyond our comprehension, O God, we fear that we are in the wrong. We think only of the consequences of misunderstanding. When our plans are disrupted, we know temporary turmoil. Fear, uncertainty, and feelings of weakness threaten. Forgive our doubting. Forgive our forgetting that you are with us through all things. Amen.

04A Hymns

"[O][Oh] Come, All Ye Faithful" Tune: ADESTE FIDELES
"Gentle Joseph, Joseph Dear" Tune: JOSEPH LIEBER, JOSEPH MEIN
"O Little Town Of Bethlehem" Tune: ST. LOUIS

Christmas Eve/Day

First Lesson: Isaiah 9:2-7
Theme: See The Light

Call To Worship

Leader: Wonderful Counselor,
People: Mighty God,
Leader: Everlasting Parent,
People: Inheritor of Peace,
All: A child has been born for us, a child has been given to us.

Collect

We come this holy night newly rejoicing in the possibility of peace throughout this world. We stand in awe before the one who offers courage for right living. We give thanks for a renewed hope of justice for all people. In your honor, O God, on this night of calm, we pause to invite the holy child to come in. Amen.

Confession

On us, who live in lands of deep darkness, you shine the light. For us, who live from day to day going our own way, you increase joy. For us, who carry all sorts of burdens, you have cracked their yoke. We confess our alleluias. Amen.

05A Hymns

"Joy To The World" Tune: ANTIOCH
"See The Little Baby" Tune: LITTLE BABY
"Silent Night" Tune: STILLE NACHT

Christmas Eve/Day

Second Lesson: Titus 2:11-14
Theme: God's Grace

Call To Worship

Here is God's grace. Here is God's salvation brought for everyone. On Christmas Eve, where fear meets hope, this holy birth is a gift from God. Come, for Christ the Savior is born.

Collect

Already, O Giver of the Gracious Gift, you teach us about simplicity with the humble birth. Salvation cannot be bought. Its only agenda is our well-being. Salvation awakens within us the answer of responsible living. Thanks be to God. Amen.

Prayer Of Confession

This Christmas we would focus on the simplicity of your grace and salvation, O God. Teach us through the life of this newborn infant to live hopeful, unpretentious lives. Let us practice self-control. Let us be honest. Let us enrich our awareness of you, O God. In celebration of the Christmas birth. Amen.

05A Hymns

"O Little Town Of Bethlehem" Tune: ST. LOUIS
"What Child Is This" Tune: GREENSLEEVES
"Silent Night, Holy Night" Tune: STILLE NACHT

Christmas Eve/Day

Gospel: Luke 2:1-14 (15-20)
Theme: Christmas

Call To Worship

Leader: Come to the manger. Come, see for yourself.
People: Holy Infant, the story is truth.
Leader: Don't keep me in a manger back then. Lift me out with your arms.
People: What would I do with you?
Leader: Let me grow. Take me with you where I can make a difference now.
People: Come into my heart, Jesus.

Collect

We burst into song at your wonderful surprises, O Wonderful God. We can contain ourselves no more than the angels could. Your realm and our life are one with this birth. Alleluia! Alleluia! Christ, Emmanuel, is born! Amen.

Prayer Of Confession

The story, O Generous God, is truth. Perhaps the first census requiring the Bethlehem trip was no coincidence. It chanced to record the family as part of history. We like the certainty of facts, O God. But now, we confess to the miracle despite our worldliness. We confess to the miracle because of our humanness. Accept our alleluia, O God. Amen.

05A Hymns

"From Heaven Above To Earth I Come" Tune: VOM HIMMEL HOCH
"Infant Holy, Infant Lowly" Tune: W ZLOBIE LEZY
"Silent Night, Holy Night" Tune: STILLE NACHT

First Sunday After Christmas (Holy Family)

First Lesson: Isaiah 63:7-9
Theme: Saving Presence

Call To Worship
Leader: Wherever we roam in car or within the heart, God is present.
People: God, our God, is with us.
Leader: God lifts us up throughout the night and in the day.
People: God, our God, is with us.
Leader: Whatever our troubles or undertakings, God is near.
All: God's nearness is a saving presence. Praise be to God.

Collect
Saving God, Protector, with grateful hearts we see the bearing of your freeing presence upon our actions, decisions, and attitudes of relationship. Through Christ. Amen.

Prayer Of Confession
The wait is over. Already we say, "Next year." Has "after Christmas" become more than a sigh of relief? What remains after the last angelic note? Guide us, God, as we carry the quiet certainty and the truth of your enduring presence within our actions. Let your truth persist in the corners of the school lunchroom, at intersections of families meeting, in the nooks of our aspirations, and within the silence of solitary times. Amen.

06A Hymns[1]
"Angels From The Realms Of Glory" Tune: REGENT SQUARE
"Who Would Think That What Was Needed" Tune: SCARLET RIB-
    BONS
"Go Tell It On The Mountain" Tune: GO TELL IT ON THE MOUN-
    TAIN

First Sunday After Christmas (Holy Family)

Second Lesson: Hebrews 2:10-18
Theme: Proclaimed Brother, Proclaimed Sister

Call To Worship
Jesus did not ask, "Will you be my brother?" or "Do you want to be my sister?" He announced, "I will proclaim your name to my brothers and sisters." Come, let us worship as the family of God because you and I are the brothers and sisters of Jesus.

Collect
You, O Compassionate God, endowed Jesus with empathy and compassion so that he might walk with us, understand us by sharing in our suffering and identify with our situations. So not only do we sense that we are his brothers and sisters, but that Jesus is our brother. Accept our gratitude for your having sent one who cares so much. Amen.

Prayer Of Confession
Let the sense of brothers and sisters in the faith become contagious, O God, so we might repair and strengthen the relationships with our siblings by birth, marriage, and adoption. Further our wanting to stand in support of our family members by trying to see things from their perspective so we also might practice mercy and faithfulness. Because of Jesus. Amen.

06A Hymns[1]
"On This Day Earth Shall Ring" Tune: PERSONENT HODIE
"Jesus, Our Brother, Strong And Good" Tune: ORIENTIS PARTIBUS
"Good Christian [Friends][Men], Rejoice" Tune: IN DULCI JUBILO

First Sunday After Christmas (Holy Family)

Gospel: Matthew 2:13-23
Theme: Protector

Call To Worship

It was not long before the sweet, idyllic night of the nativity took flight. God stayed in touch with Joseph. Joseph, the alert, steady protector, kept his family on a run of flight, escape, and return. Let us learn from God's choice of Joseph.

Collect

Help us, Protecting God, to be like Joseph, who took seriously his parental care of the little boy who was also God's Son. Help us to balance the ideal with the real, the resourceful with the practical. Always, lead us to stay in touch with you even as you reach out for us. In Jesus' name. Amen.

Prayer Of Confession

Even on our long flights away from danger and into safe territory, you remain with us, O God. Do you have a plan for our lives as resolutely to be fulfilled and carried out by us as Joseph cared for the holy infant? Guide us toward stretching our capacity single-mindedly and faithfully to tend our responsibilities. In Jesus' name. Amen.

06A Hymns[1]

"Go Tell It On The Mountain" Tune: GO TELL IT ON THE MOUNTAIN
"Sing A Different Song" Tune: DIFFERENT SONG
"There's A Song In The Air" Tune: CHRISTMAS SONG

---

1. To echo the season, on the two Sundays of Christmas sing the refrain to "O Come, O Come, Emmanuel" as a benediction response.

Second Sunday After Christmas

First Lesson: Jeremiah 31:7-14
Theme: Like A Watered Garden

Call To Worship

Have you ever watched a dry, limp-leafed garden spring back to life after a good drink of water? Such is the vitality God's care will give to your drooping spirits. Come, walk by winter streams of living water. Drink your fill and know renewal of life because of God, whose action says to each of us, "As far as I am concerned, you count."

Collect

We are here, O God, because we want you to lead us back onto the path of life. You show us that your plan is to save us from the coldest times of our souls. Your concern awakens within us a radiance that thaws frozen hearts. Amen.

Prayer Of Confession

In the cold and winter of our being awaits a spring of possibility. Hearten our remembering, O God, that the seed of hope lies present within us — resting, refueling, holding on. Help us to be strong during the times our hope pauses so that our waiting will announce trust. In the name of Jesus. Amen.

07A Hymns

"God Is Working His Purpose Out" Tune: PURPOSE
"Hymn Of Promise" or "In The Bulb There Is A Flower" Tune: PROMISE
"All People That On Earth Do Dwell" Tune: OLD HUNDREDTH

Second Sunday After Christmas

Second Lesson: Ephesians 1:3-14
Theme: Marked With The Seal

Call To Worship

God has marked us, O people, with the seal of the Holy Spirit. Blessed be the God and Parent of our Savior Jesus Christ, who has blessed us in Christ with every spiritual blessing, just as God chose us in Christ before the worlds began to be holy and blameless in love. Let us rise to this blessing and do honor to these wonder-filled words of life. In the name of our Savior. Amen.

Collect

To you, O God, who exists before time, through time, and beyond time, we rejoice. You are a redeeming God, who saves us through Christ. You are a forgiving God, who forgives us through Christ. You are a gracious God, who lavishes your grace on us. Let us live in a way that praises you, O God. Amen.

Prayer Of Confession

We look back, O God, and see your hand in our life. Remind us today of your continuing presence so we might trust in you in all life to come. In the name of Jesus. Amen.

07A Hymns

"Angels Holy, High And Lowly" Tune: LLANHERNE
"God Of Our Life, Through All The Circling Years" Tune: SANDON
"Sing Them Over Again To Me" Tune: WORDS OF LIFE

Second Sunday After Christmas

Gospel: John 1:(1-9) 10-18
Theme: Begin Again

Call To Worship

Leader: In the beginning, God saw that the world was good. Let us also sing the song of life. Begin again in the new year as God started fresh with the creation of Jesus.

People: In this beginning, God sees that the world is still good. Let us praise God.

Collect

We wait for the newness of life that will unfold. We relish a fresh start while cherishing the layers of living we have experienced. We welcome your new creation, O God. Amen.

Prayer Of Confession

Leader: Ever-creating God, always giving, always forgiving, hear your people when we call.

People: Hear us, God, when dread or apprehension curbs our fortitude in a world that seldom remains the same.

Leader: Forgive our thinking that you have finished with us.

People: Hear us, God, when life changes and fluctuations threaten our capacity to adapt.

All: Let us recognize the spirit of your presence with a new spirit of greeting what comes our way. Amen.

07A Hymns

"Joyful, Joyful, We Adore [Thee][You]" Tune: HYMN TO JOY
"This Is A Day Of New Beginnings" Tune: BEGINNINGS
"Love Divine, All Loves Excelling" Tune: BEECHER or HYFRYDOL

Epiphany Of Our Lord

First Lesson: Isaiah 60:1-6
Theme: God's Light

Call To Worship

Leader: Epiphany is about God's surprises.
Epiphany is about a dawning, God's unfolding.
Epiphany is about the bursting forth of God's light.

People: Surprise us, God.
Let light enter our uncertainty.
Let us see afresh the ancient truths.
Let us surprise ourselves with understanding.

All: **Come, let us worship God.**

Collect

We come to you, O God, recognizing that part of Epiphany's surprise includes discovery. A piece of discovery carries shock. A slice of what is new brings wonder. Let the radiance of your Epiphany light cause us, reflectively, to arise and shine. Amen.

Prayer Of Confession

God, forgive us when we are in the limelight for the wrong reasons. Help us discern between self-centering and casting light upon God. Let the times we receive public attention be for the right reasons: to live in God's light. Amen.

08A Hymns[1]

"As With Gladness [Those][Men] Of Old" Tune: DIX
"Now Let Every Tongue Adore Thee" Tune: WACHET AUF
"Arise, Your Light Has Come" Tune: FESTAL SONG

Epiphany Of Our Lord

Second Lesson: Ephesians 3:1-12
Theme: Divine Mystery

Call To Worship
Consider the mysteries of Christ and God. So little do we understand about the source of our being, the initial spark of creation in the world, the gift of Jesus, the depth of God's love for persons one by one, the re-creation of the human spirit. So little do we need to understand. Let us worship the source of all being.

Collect
You are a God of surprises, O Great Creator. How are we to respond to these divine life mysteries? With quiet marvel, in wonder, with awe, with surprise, and with acceptance. Amen.

Prayer Of Confession
As we study the intricate body system that converts nourishing food into sustaining energy, we marvel at your creation, O God. As we experience the conversion of spiritual nourishment into renewal of hope, our gratitude soars. As we examine medical and scientific developments because of human intellect, we stand in awe of you. As novel ideas come seemingly from nowhere, we smile with surprise. We see the epiphany of your amazing creative hand in all of creation, O God. Amen.

08A Hymns[1]
"Of The [Father's Love][Parent's Heart] Begotten" Tune: DIVINUM
    MYSTERIUM
"Spirit Of God, Descend Upon My Heart" Tune: MORECAMBE
"Creation's Lord, We Give Thee Thanks" Tune: RAMWOLD

31

Epiphany Of Our Lord

Gospel: Matthew 2:1-12
Theme: Homage

Call To Worship

What gifts would you bring to Jesus? Where do you look for Jesus today? Is your respect more than lip service? How do you pay homage to him?

Collect

We show you respect, O Living Savior, by how we treat work associates, parents, teachers, students, life partners, and all others we meet daily. We honor you when we assess ourselves as valid, worthy parts of your creation. We bring you homage when we recognize you at unexpected crossroads. Amen.

Prayer Of Confession

Forgive us, O God, when we leave you in the manger and put you away with the Christmas decorations for another year. Amen.

08A Hymns[1]

"We Three Kings" Tune: KINGS OF ORIENT
"The First Nowell" Tune: THE FIRST NOWELL
"Amen, Amen" Tune: AMEN

---

1. As a reminder of the John 1 reading from Christmas 2, sing verse 1 of "This Is The Day" as an opening response during the Epiphany season. Congregations and choirs enjoy singing this antiphonally with the congregation echoing the choir's lead.

Baptism Of Our Lord

First Lesson: Isaiah 42:1-9
Theme: Chosen

Call To Worship

Leader: What brings you to this place today?
People: Knowing that we too are chosen, we come as people seeking strength and courage.
Leader: May God be with you in your search.
People: May God be with us all.

Collect

The echo of Jesus' baptism resounds in our own baptism. So close is God to us — God who gives breath and spirit to those who walk on earth. God has taken us by the hand, both as God's chosen and as those in whom God's soul delights. Amen.

Prayer Of Confession

Holy Creator, Parent, give us the boldness to greet the touch of your hand with an eager step. Persist, O God, when you declare to us your promises and our actions hint, "So what?" Give us the determination to avoid lagging behind as we feel the pull of rebellion. Help us quiet the defiance of not wanting to be held accountable. Keep us from dodging the responsibilities of having been chosen as your people. Amen.

09A Hymns

"[All][He] Who Would Valiant Be" Tune: ST. DUNSTAN'S
"[O Morning Star How Fair And Bright][How Brightly Shines The Morning Star]" Tune: WIE SCHÖN LEUCHTET
"Lord Of All Hopefulness" or "Be [Now][Thou] My Vision" Tune: SLANE

Baptism Of Our Lord

Second Lesson: Acts 10:34-43
Theme: Unbiased

Call To Worship

Leader: God shows no partiality in accepting us. Anyone, anywhere, who believes in God and does what is right when the choice of doing good or evil presents itself, is acceptable to God.

People: That includes us.

Leader: That includes us. It also includes those with views differing from ours,

People: And those with whom we utterly disagree.

All: God is God of us all.

Collect

We are here, O God, to learn more about the law of love. Teach us so we will be stronger in choosing love over disdain, acceptance over rejection, tolerance over prejudice, and right over wrong. In Jesus' name. Amen.

Prayer Of Confession

Forgive us, God, when we act as if we were an exclusive club. We would like to be as fair and accepting as Jesus, but usually our ways are not your ways. We hate to give in and forgive others. Sometimes forgiveness seems impossible. Help us follow Jesus' example. In his name. Amen.

09A Hymns

"All Hail The Power of Jesus' Name" Tune: CORONATION or MILES LANE

"Your Ways Are Not Our Own" Tune: SCHUMANN

"Once To Ev'ry Man And Nation" Tune: EBENEZER

Baptism Of Our Lord

Gospel: Matthew 3:13-17
Theme: Baptized

Call To Worship

Leader: You are baptized.
People: Baptized — launched to begin, to start afresh, to initiate.
Leader: Baptized — part of God's one, faithful family.
People: Baptized — acceptance because of God's love.
Leader: Baptized — beloved.
People: Baptized — acknowledgment by those who care about me that I am God's own dear child.
Leader: We are baptized — freed, saved for new life in Christ.

Collect

Jesus, who opened the way for our baptism, you, first, were baptized. You, first, were the one to whom God said, "This is my Son, the Beloved, with whom I am well pleased." How beautiful at baptisms we witness in this place, dear God, that we hear the echo of your voice saying, "This is my child, my beloved, with whom I am well pleased." Amen.

Prayer Of Confession

Gracious, Loving God, we pray that all our lives will be renewed and reaffirmed when one is baptized. This simple symbol of living water stretches far beyond what we speak with words. In the name of the Triune God. Amen.

09A Hymns

"I Know Not How" Tune: BANGOR
"Into My Heart, Lord Jesus" Response
"That King Before Whose Majesty" Tune: OLD HUNDREDTH

Second Sunday After Epiphany

First Lesson: Isaiah 49:1-7
Theme: From Your Beginning

Call To Worship

Leader: Before you were born, the Creator knew about you and named you as God's own. From your beginning, God has been your strength. You are chosen to be God's light to other people. Your charge is to tell by what you say and what you do that our saving God is active in your life and in theirs.

People: Come, let us worship the God of our strength and of our salvation.

Collect

O God, the source of our being, we come now into closer relationship with you. Grant us inquiring minds so we may learn about you. Grant us receptive hearts so your spirit can make us new. Open our ears so your plans will get through to us. Amen.

Prayer Of Confession

When all is well, Creator God, it is easy to suppose our accomplishments are entirely our own. We take the credit. When we get into trouble, quiet our gloom. Remind us always of your supporting partnership with us through Christ. Amen.

10A Hymns

"Let Us [All] With A Gladsome Mind" or "As The Sun Doth Daily Rise" Tune: INNOCENTS

"Lead Us, O Father" Tune: LANGRAN

"Come, Holy Spirit, Heavenly Dove" or "Jesus, United By Thy Grace" Tune: ST. AGNES

Second Sunday After Epiphany

Second Lesson: 1 Corinthians 1:1-9
Theme: Enriched

Call To Worship
Enriched bread is improved. It is fortified with nutrients and boosted with power to give energy to our strength. In every way, the Apostle Paul says, we have been enriched in Jesus Christ who will strengthen us to the end. Consider today how your life has been empowered by Jesus Christ. What nourishment for your spirit fortifies you? What strength have you gained?

Collect
Faithful Sustainer, you are the source of our strength. You, who continually call us into Christ's neighborhood, strengthen us for speaking up for what is right. In Jesus' name. Amen.

Prayer Of Confession
Turn us around, O God, from devouring quick fix junk food for the soul. Lead us, rather, to the vegetables and complex carbohydrates that you offer for the nourishment of a solid faith. Through Jesus. Amen.

10A Hymns
"God [Himself Is][Is Truly] With Us" Tune: ARNSBERG
"Come, Gracious Spirit, Heavenly Dove" Tune: MENDON
"Great Is [Thy][Your] Faithfulness" Tune: FAITHFULNESS

Second Sunday After Epiphany

Gospel: John 1:29-42
Theme: Come And See

Call To Worship

Come and see. There's a person you've got to know. There's someone you must meet. If you dare to, follow him. Be as Andrew, bring yourself. Then lead another to him. Be a Simon Peter and follow. Come and see.

Collect

Whet the appetite of our soul, O God, so we might recognize you when we see you. Through Christ. Amen.

Prayer Of Confession

How can we know you, when no one has ever seen God? Teach us to trust within our heart of hearts that we will know you and will follow. In Jesus' name. Amen.

10A Hymns

"[O][Oh] Worship The King, All Glorious Above" or "We Worship You, God" Tune: LYONS
"We Would See Jesus" Tune: CUSHMAN
"We Meet You, O Christ" Tune: STANLEY BEACH

Third Sunday After Epiphany

First Lesson: Isaiah 9:1-4
Theme: Out Of Darkness

Call To Worship

Leader: "There will be no gloom for those who were in anguish," says the writer of Isaiah.

People: Blessed be Almighty God.

Leader: It is God who comes to draw us out of darkness with a great light.

People: Praise be to God.

Collect

A note from God to all who live in a land of deep darkness, who live with intractable pain, who do not have enough food to eat, who live in mental torment, who seem only to fail: Into your darkness, dear people, God's light will shine. Amen.

Prayer Of Confession

You know, O God, about our varieties of anguish. Your beautiful words say there will be no gloom for those who *were* in anguish. We hear your promise that suffering is not forever. We are grateful. Amen.

11A Hymns

"Ye Watchers And Ye Holy Ones" Tune: LASST UNS ERFREUEN
"My Master, See, The Time Has Come" Tune: MORNING SONG
"Now Bless The God Of Israel" Tune: FOREST GREEN

Third Sunday After Epiphany

Second Lesson: 1 Corinthians 1:10-18
Theme: In Christ's Name

Call To Worship
Come and worship the one true God. Let us put away divisive attitudes. Let us avoid idolizing those whose charisma draws our attention and upstages Jesus. Let us strive for single-minded purpose that generates unity.

Collect
In your name we pray, O Christ. We would stay centered on your person, your example, and your teachings. We would follow your way of life as best we can. We would be a community of believers who work together. For your sake. Amen.

Prayer Of Confession
We can become so enthusiastic about the faith, O God, that zeal overtakes us. Teach us to release and abandon our own agendas that threaten to get in the way of deepening the community of believers. For the sake of Jesus. Amen.

11A Hymns
"Now Thank We All Our God" Tune: NUN DANKET
"In The Cross Of Christ I Glory" Tune: RATHBUN
"O Jesus, I Have Promised" Tune: ANGEL'S STORY

Third Sunday After Epiphany

Gospel: Matthew 4:12-23
Theme: Follow

Call To Worship

Leader: Enter this place as practicing Christians.
People: We would be more loving.
Leader: Enter this place to prepare.
People: We would be more holy.
Leader: Enter this place to pray.
People: We would be like Jesus.
Leader: Enter this place to listen.

Collect

Open our hearts, O God, to grow in understanding that this place is greater than one more organization to cubbyhole our time. Teach us how to be wholehearted Christians. Teach us how to follow Jesus. Amen.

Prayer Of Confession

God, who asks us to drop everything and follow, we cannot just drop everything and follow. Will we be lesser Christians? We have families to feed. Too much to do. We need to fit being Christian into the convenience of other plans. No matter how thin our efforts to follow you, please accept them. Do not give up on us. Cheer us to refrain from abandoning ourselves. Amen.

11A Hymns

"Stand Up, Stand Up For Jesus," "Remember God Was Guiding," or "Now Is The Time Approaching" Tune: WEBB
"Amazing Grace" Tune: AMAZING GRACE
"Lord, I Want To Be A Christian" Tune: I WANT TO BE A CHRISTIAN

41

Fourth Sunday After Epiphany

First Lesson: Micah 6:1-8
Theme: Do Justice

Call To Worship
Discrimination, favoritism, inequity, inequality, partiality, prejudice, unfairness — these are the words of injustice. God requires of us that we do justice. Hear the call to turn around injury. Hear the call to do what is right. Come, let us worship God.

Collect
Awaken us to action, O God. Let us do justice by being just. Let us do justice by paying attention to the special needs of specific people. Let us break down injustice into manageable pieces. Let us speak up for what is right. Awaken us to action, O God. Amen.

Prayer Of Confession
Dear God, rather than practice justice, we dismiss injustice as too pervasive for any one of us to overcome. We like to keep justice beyond our fingertips, to distance it as an impossible ideal. Let us search our hearts for ways we contribute to injustice. Open us to perceive what is unfair. Help us to be human wedges who split apart injustice wherever we recognize it. Amen.

12A Hymns
"O God Of Earth And Altar" or "O God Of Every Nation" Tune: LLANGLOFFAN
"Let Justice Flow Like Streams" Tune: ST. THOMAS
"[God The Omnipotent][Christ The Victorious]" Tune: RUSSIAN HYMN

Fourth Sunday After Epiphany

Second Lesson: 1 Corinthians 1:18-31
Theme: God's Foolishness

Call To Worship

Leader: The Creator chose not to use the route of wisdom to make God known to a select few. God preferred the path of belief so that all might know God. God chose to come to us through what is weak in the world. All can identify with the defenseless newborn infant.

People: A baby's weakness is also its strength. To survive, a baby must trust and a baby is able to trust.

Collect

You, O God, chose what is foolish in the world to shame the wise. You chose what is weak in the world to shame the strong. You chose what is low and despised in the world so we would realize that you, not we, are the source of our life. To you, O God, we give the praise. Through Christ. Amen.

Prayer Of Confession

Belief in you, O God, has little to do with the wisdom of Ph.D.s, sheltered workshops, trade school certificates, or bachelor or professional degrees. We can neither buy nor argue our belief in you. We cannot even boast about our capacity to believe. At best, despite all our efforts, only can we allow belief to slip in, to happen. Through Christ. Amen.

12A Hymns

"Immortal, Invisible, God Only Wise" Tune: ST. DENIO
"God Of Earth And Sea And Heaven" Tune: HYFRYDOL or LLANSANNAN
"I Sing The Mighty Power Of God" Tune: ELLACOMBE

43

Fourth Sunday After Epiphany

Gospel: Matthew 5:1-12
Theme: Blessed

Call To Worship

Leader: Blessed are you poor in spirit, for yours is the realm of God.
People: Blessed are we who mourn, for we will be comforted.
Leader: Blessed are you meek, for you will inherit the earth.
People: Blessed are we who hunger and thirst for righteousness, for we will be filled.
Leader: Blessed are you merciful, for you will receive mercy.
Men: Blessed are the pure in heart, for we will see God.
Leader: Blessed are you peacemakers, for you will be called children of God.
Women: Blessed are we who are persecuted for righteousness' sake, for ours is the realm of God.
Leader: Blessed are you when people revile you and persecute you and utter all kinds of evil against you falsely because of Jesus.
All: Rejoice and be glad, for the reward is great.

Collect

When you bless us, O God, you restore our sense of well-being and tell us we are on the right track. When you bless us, you bring us together with the holy. Amen.

Prayer Of Confession

Gracious God, as we live as best we can, let us know your blessing. In the name of Christ. Amen.

12A Hymns

"Praise, My Soul, The King Of Heaven" Tune: PRAISE MY SOUL
"Blest Are The Pure In Heart" Tune: FRANCONIA
"Blessed Are The Poor In Spirit" Tune: ANNIKA'S DANCE

Fifth Sunday After Epiphany

First Lesson: Isaiah 58:1-9a (9b-12)
Theme: Draw Near

Call To Worship

Leader: Draw near to God, you who seek God and want to know God's ways.

People: How do we draw near to God?

Leader: Not by doing hurtful things to your body to gain God's or anyone else's attention.

People: How, then, do we draw near?

Leader: Not by humbling yourself at another's expense.

People: Is it possible to come closer to God?

Leader: Yes, God will hear your voice as you do things that increase the well-being of others.

Collect

We come, O God, to serve your interests and not our own. Amen.

Prayer Of Confession

Gracious God, strengthen us to look outward rather than inward so we might see and respond to the distress of a needy world. Help us to loosen the knots of injustice and oppression. Help us to share what we have with the impoverished. Remind us to stay in touch with the needs of relatives. Then, O God, you will hear our voices and see that we also have what we need. Amen.

13A Hymns

"Lead On, [Eternal Sovereign][O King Eternal]" Tune: LANCASHIRE
"O God Of Love, O God Of Peace" Tune: HESPERUS
"Let There Be Light, Lord God Of Hosts" Tune: ELTON or PENTE-COST

Fifth Sunday After Epiphany

Second Lesson: 1 Corinthians 2:1-12 (13-16)
Theme: Truly Human, Truly God's

Call To Worship
Epiphany surprise also contains the wonder of mystery. "For what human being knows what is truly human except the human spirit that is within? So also no one comprehends what is truly God's except the Spirit of God." Come to worship always ready to be surprised and awed by the gifts of the Spirit that God offers us.

Collect
Slowly, as your Spirit searches and knows us through and through, O God, we come to sense not only your depth but the depth of the human spirit. Amen.

Prayer Of Confession
We come, O Spirit of the Living God, ready for your Spirit to make a difference in our lives. Whisper to us from tomorrow as well as from yesterday. Fill us with the truth of your Spirit. Shape us and use us as your own, O Spirit of the Living God. Amen.

13A Hymns
"Spirit, Spirit Of Gentleness" Tune: SPIRIT
"Send Down Thy Truth, O God" Tune: ST. MICHAEL
"Spirit Of The Living God, Fall Afresh On Me" Tune: IVERSON

Fifth Sunday After Epiphany

Gospel: Matthew 5:13-20
Theme: Lifting The Lamp Shade

Call To Worship

Leader: Let your light shine in such a way that others may see your good works and give the glory to God. Come, let us worship together.

People: Come, let us worship.

Collect

God, who is light and who brings light to the world, you clarify our path. We rejoice in the truth of your light. We rejoice in the persistence of your light. We rejoice in the hope your light brings through Christ. Amen.

Prayer Of Confession

God of light, we would bring your illumination to all in the house. When we hesitate, nudge us toward peeking out from beneath our lamp shades. Encourage us to keep our eyes open when the light seems too bright. Remind us that you remain with us, clarifying and illustrating through the example of Jesus the Christ. Amen.

13A Hymns

"[Sing Praise To God, Who Has Shaped][Praise To The Lord]" Tune: LOBE DEN HERREN

"This Little Light Of Mine" Tune: LATTIMER

"Arise, Your Light Is Come" or "Rise Up, O [Church][Men] Of God" Tune: FESTAL SONG

Sixth Sunday After Epiphany

First Lesson: Deuteronomy 30:15-20
Theme: Choose Life

Call To Worship

Leader: Choose life
People: Even when all meaning seems to have drained from your life.
Leader: Choose life
People: Even when you must contend with disease, a chronic condition, or economic perils.
Leader: Choose life
People: Even when the loss of a relationship or death of a lifemate or a child muddles your whole being.
Leader: Choose life
People: Even when life changes bring unsettling hours.
All: Yes, even when ... choose life.

Collect

We would live as fully and meaningfully as possible, O God. Enliven our senses to be aware of the beauty of the world around us, our relationships, and within our own being. Amen.

Prayer Of Confession

Sometimes, God, everything seems too much effort, too much trouble, or futile. Then we need your words: Choose life. When it is our turn to be doleful, remind us to choose life so we may live fully rather than waste prized time. Amen.

14A Hymns

"When Morning Gilds The Skies" Tune: LAUDES DOMINI
"[If Thou But Suffer God To Guide Thee][If You But Trust In God To Guide You]" Tune: NEUMARK [WER NUR DEN LIEBEN GOTT]
"Rejoice, [You][Ye] Pure In Heart" Tune: MARION

Sixth Sunday After Epiphany

Second Lesson: 1 Corinthians 3:1-9
Theme: Servanthood

Call To Worship
We are God's servants, working together. It is God who gives the growth. We are God's field, God's building. This is the essence of the life of this church. Let us be about the work of God.

Collect
You, O God, have plans for us that we have not yet imagined. You, who inspires the life within a seed to grow, also inspire the vitality of this congregation. Praise be to you, O God. Amen.

Prayer Of Confession
Quiet our twinges of human jealousy, O God. Silence our quarreling even if it is only a grumble. Turn our hearts away from finding fault. Let nothing distract us from the service this church can offer. Guide our congregation toward the shaping of common goals that reflect the discovery of your plans for our church. Through Christ. Amen.

14A Hymns
"[Incarnate][Strong Son Of] God, Immortal Love" Tune: ROCK-INGHAM
"We Are Not Our Own" Tune: YARNTON
"For The Beauty Of The Earth" Tune: DIX

Sixth Sunday After Epiphany

Gospel: Matthew 5:21-37
Theme: The Mere Thought Of It

Call To Worship
Consider how different the world would be if we took care of sores of the heart before they became ulcers. How different things would be if we attended to small grievances before they snowballed into lawsuits. How different if love and kindness were to prevail.

Collect
It is the little stuff of not loving, dear God — the insult, the snide remark, an old and submerged anger simmering within, the unsettled relationship — that corrodes the soul. Help us to take care of unfinished concerns of the heart. Draw us toward reconciliation. In Jesus' name. Amen.

Prayer Of Confession
We admit, O God, that the mere thought of some things is enough to send us down the wrong path. Guide us back to the laws of kindness, of forgiveness, and of a loving spirit that lead to fullness of life. In Jesus' name. Amen.

14A Hymns
"Awake, My Soul, And With The Sun" Tune: MORNING HYMN
"O For A World" Tune: AZMON
"Where Charity And Love Prevail"[1] Tune: ST. PETER

---

1. Sing "Where Charity And Love Prevail" antiphonally with "In Christ There Is No East Or West" as a choir/congregation duet.

50

Seventh Sunday After Epiphany

First Lesson: Leviticus 19:1-2, 9-18
Theme: Not Just On Sunday

Call To Worship

Leader: Come, let us give thanks to God, let us talk to God in prayer
and listen for the word of God which transforms failure and
death into hope and life. We come to worship God, recognizing that while we were created in the image of God, we
are not God. God is in charge of all creation. Our lives are
gifts of God.

People: In response, we seek to live with an attitude of faith.

Collect

Fortify us, God, for the days that fall between Sundays that we
might practice being holy. Increase our understanding of being holy
as more than engaging in a vertical relationship with you. Let us
enlarge holiness to encompass the horizontal dimension of the cross,
that is, how we are with each other. Amen.

Prayer Of Confession

Gathered here, Gracious God, we feel strong enough to continue
on the path of holiness. After we return to daily living, our determination slackens. Give us courage and the strength of integrity to close
the gap between living a holy life in theory and practicing it. Amen.

15A Hymns

"Holy, Holy, Holy" Tune: NICAEA
"More Love To [Thee][You], O Christ" Tune: MORE LOVE TO YOU
"Jesus Call Us" Tune: GALILEE **OR** "Called As Partners In Christ's
Service" Tune: BEECHER

Seventh Sunday After Epiphany

Second Lesson: 1 Corinthians 3:10-11, 16-23
Theme: Groundwork

Call To Worship

Leader: We are layers of foundations shaped by our deeds and our
words.

**People: We have come to hear God's word. Let the message of
Christ's model influence our actions as we lay foundations based on Jesus Christ.**

Collect

Be near, O God, as we take more than a glance at the patterns
within our relationships. Help us to see clearly how our words, actions, and attitudes influence the foundations forming in our children,
our students, and others who observe us unnoticed. In Christ we pray.
Amen.

Prayer Of Confession

Merciful God, forgive our discouragement those times we become
acutely aware of our imperfections. We are capable of dissecting our
failings until nothing is left to honor. By your grace, help us balance
our shortfalls by persistently greeting the new day of trying. Amen.

15A Hymns

"Christ Is Made The Sure Foundation" Tune: REGENT SQUARE
"Come [Down][Forth], O Love Divine" Tune: DOWN AMPNEY
"The Church's One Foundation" Tune: AURELIA

Seventh Sunday After Epiphany

Gospel: Matthew 5:38-48
Theme: Perfect

Call To Worship
Jesus' teachings challenge us to live fully within the law of Christian love. Come, let us gain strength for the journey.

Collect
We come to this place of new beginnings, O God. Here we remember our failings and know the freedom to move on. Here we find renewal of faith and hope in you, O God. Here faith in ourselves and hope for ourselves meet your grace. Amen.

Prayer Of Confession
Leader: Jesus said, If anyone strikes you on the right cheek, turn the other also.

People: But, God, if I wait around, they might kill me.

Leader: And if anyone wants to sue you and take your coat, give him your athletic jacket as well.

People: But, God, some people do not deserve my coat.

Leader: And if anyone forces you to go one mile, go also the second mile.

People: But, God, I will not be a slave.

Leader: Give to everyone who begs from you, and do not refuse anyone who wants to borrow from you.

People: But, God, I'll never see it again.

Leader: Love your enemies and pray for those who persecute you.

People: Do I have to? I hate them.

Leader: Be perfect.

People: How can I possibly be perfect, O God, when I am so human?

Leader: Hush, God knows that. There is a wideness in God's mercy that you would not believe.

15A Hymns
"Teach Me, My God And King" Tune: MORNINGTON
"This Is A Day Of New Beginnings" Tune: BEGINNINGS
"There's A Wideness In God's Mercy" Tune: WELLESLEY

Eighth Sunday After Epiphany

First Lesson: Isaiah 49:8-16a
Theme: I Will Not Forget You

Call To Worship
Sing for joy, O heavens, and exult, O earth; break forth, O mountains, into singing! For God has comforted God's people, and God will have compassion on the suffering ones. Sing for joy, O people, for God will not forget you.

Collect
God has kept us. God has not thrown us away. Furthermore, from paths to highways, God has made all kinds of roads to guide us through the mountainous ranges of our lives. God remembers us. Be joyful before almighty God. Amen.

Prayer Of Confession
Almighty God, who has written our names on the palm of your hand, we put our trust in you. Those dark moments we believe you have forgotten us, remind us that you are on our side forever. Amen.

16A Hymns
"O Be Joyful In The Lord" Tune: FINLAY or ROCK OF AGES
"How Gentle God's Commands" Tune: DENNIS
"Be [Calm][Still], My Soul" Tune: FINLANDIA

Eighth Sunday After Epiphany

Second Lesson: 1 Corinthians 4:1-5
Theme: God's Commendation

Call To Worship

Commendation from God is God's approval, endorsement, and praise. We, who are trying to be trustworthy Christians, will receive commendation from God. God will reveal the purposes of our hearts in God's time. So forget about the judgment others pass on us now. It is God whose opinion counts.

Collect

If God will vouch for our good efforts even after bringing to our attention the bad news about our lives, then we indeed should feel encouraged to keep trying at this life as a Christian. For Jesus' sake. Amen.

Prayer Of Confession

You tell us not even to judge ourselves, dear God. That is difficult because we are prone to err. Remind us of the freedom we know when we live first from the base of your affirmation. Remind us of how little energy we waste when we pay attention to the clean purposes of our hearts. In Jesus' name. Amen.

16A Hymns

"O Day Of God, Draw Nigh" Tune: ST. MICHAEL
"How Like A Gentle Spirit" Tune: SURSUM CORDA
"Take My Life [God,][And] Let It Be" Tune: VIENNA

Eighth Sunday After Epiphany

Gospel: Matthew 6:24-34
Theme: As Birds Of The Air

Call To Worship
Over-wintering cardinals put spirit into February existence. Their exuberant song cannot wait for dawn to spill into the air. Trusting, they seem not to worry but go actively and fully about the tasks of their day. At dusk, their last act, of course, is the creation of another song. Consider God's provision for the birds of the air and rejoice in God's care of us.

Collect
You know what we need, Holy Parent, even before we do. You provide for the nourishment of our lives, almost before we have noticed. So let the warbling of our souls find voice. Amen.

Prayer Of Confession
Let us lay aside fretting and use our energy for sustaining and constructive matters such as unreserved singing within our souls. Amen.

16A Hymns
"[Be Not Dismayed][God Will Take Care Of You]" Tune: MARTIN
"Thus Far You Have Led Us" Tune: KREMSER
"Holy Spirit, [Light][Truth] Divine" Tune: CANTERBURY

Transfiguration Of Our Lord

First Lesson: Exodus 24:12-18
Theme: Into And Out Of The Clouds

Call To Worship

Clouds of confusion, clouds hiding our path, clouds making unclear the direction our life is to proceed. Then the clearing — lifting of the fog, clarity of purpose, keen sight, the new course. Is this not also our story of journey up the hill? Our story of change? Of resolve? Come, let us worship.

Collect

We go into and come out of many clouds in a lifetime, dear God. Each time, we are changed, transformed. Each time, we emerge a different person. Thank you for meeting us in the foggy places, for walking through the clouds with us, and leading us into the clearing. Amen.

Prayer Of Confession

Did you just wait and wait in the foothills of the mountain, Moses, during those six long days before God called to you? And what about your lengthy stay on the mountain? Teach us, Holy God, like Moses, to have patience to wait for your call and to work things out. Call to us from within the clouds of our confusion. Encourage us, like Moses, to be brave enough to venture where we can see nothing as far as a footstep. Amen.

18A Hymns

"The God Of Abraham Praise" Tune: LEONI
"God Be In My Head" Tune: LYTLINGTON
"[God][Lord], Speak To Me That I May Speak" Tune: CANONBURY

Transfiguration Of Our Lord

Second Lesson: 2 Peter 1:16-21
Theme: God's Own

Call To Worship

Leader: It is God who calls us as God's own.
It is God who has plans for us.
It is God who confers upon us honor and respect.
Come, let us worship God.

People: Let us worship God together.

Collect

Affirming God, just as your blessing of Jesus at the transfiguration changed him forever in the hearts of his disciples, we notice how differently we see others when we recognize your approval both of them and of us. Seeing that we are not the authors but are the receivers of your blessing, we bow in humility. In Christ we pray. Amen.

Prayer Of Confession

With prayers of confusion, we express bewilderment about who is in charge of our lives. With prayers of profession, we affirm your movement in our lives. We are grateful, O God, whenever we recognize the Holy Spirit moving within us. Let us live with the integrity of knowing we are your cherished ones. Through Christ. Amen.

18A Hymns

"I Love To Tell The Story" Tune: HANKEY

"In The Bulb There Is A Flower" or "Hymn Of Promise" Tune: PROMISE

"[We Have Come At Christ's Own Bidding][God The Spirit, Guide And Guardian][Praise The Lord! Ye Heavens, Adore Him]" Tune: HYFRYDOL

Transfiguration Of Our Lord

Gospel: Matthew 17:1-9
Theme: Constancy Amid Change

Call To Worship

God said it again. At the transfiguration of Jesus, God said, "This is my Son, the Beloved; with him I am well pleased." God had said these same words at Jesus' baptism. After all Jesus' living, all his work, and all his teaching, the mind of God did not change. Come, let us worship this God whose love is constant.

Collect

Though life may alter us radically, so much so that we hardly know ourselves and seem like strangers to our friends, you still know us, Merciful God. You still are pleased with what you see. Thanks be to you, O God. Amen.

Prayer Of Confession

Could it be, O God, that you will never change your mind about loving us, no matter how we change? Because of Jesus. Amen.

18A Hymns

"Christ, Whose Glory Fills The Skies" Tune: RATISBON
"The King Shone In His Beauty" Tune: PASSION CHORALE
"[Incarnate God][Strong Son Of God], Immortal Love" Tune: ROCKINGHAM

Ash Wednesday

First Lesson: Joel 2:1-2, 12-17
Theme: Return To Me

Call To Worship
It is Ash Wednesday, the time to return to God from wherever we have wandered in spirit. Let people of all ages return to the community of God with wholehearted vigor. Return to me, says our God, for God is gracious and merciful and slow to anger. God abounds in steadfast love and relents from punishing.

Collect
As we walk with Jesus through these forty days and forty nights, we would become more like Jesus. Make us more holy, O God. Make us more humble and more faithful because of Jesus. Amen.

Prayer Of Confession
Thoughts about Ash Wednesday and the beginning of Lent set off an inner alarm of darkness and gloom, O God. We remember Jesus' long journey through Lent to the cross. Lead us gently toward our own meditative journeys, because we would rather skip over the searching time of growth and leap quickly to Easter joy. Amen.

19A Hymns[1]
"Lord, Who Throughout These Forty Days" Tune: LAND OF REST
"Sunday's Palms Are Wednesday's Ashes" Tune: BEACH SPRING
"Lord, Make Me More Holy" Tune: LORD, MAKE ME MORE HOLY

Ash Wednesday

Second Lesson: 2 Corinthians 5:20b—6:10
Theme: Reconcile

Call To Worship

How does the way you live champion yourself to God? Ash Wednesday is the time to begin looking at how we live out the Christian way both in our inner life and in the world.

Collect

Lent is a time, dear God, that we come particularly close to you. Remembering these weeks of struggle in Jesus' life, we listen more closely for your kind presence within our silence and throughout our babel. We sense that you are also listening to us and encouraging us to live in a manner that brings us closer to your hope for us. Amen.

Prayer Of Confession

Help us, merciful and gracious God, to reconcile ourselves to the way you would have us live. In the name of Jesus. Amen.

19A Hymns[1]

"Beneath The Cross Of Jesus" Tune: ST. CHRISTOPHER
"Father In Heaven, Who Lovest All" Tune: HESPERUS or SAXBY
"Were You There?" Tune: WERE YOU THERE

Ash Wednesday

Gospel: Matthew 6:1-6, 16-21
Theme: Look At Me!

Call To Worship

Ash Wednesday begins a period of reflection. Let us remember that reflection is active pondering about the meaning of our lives, the life of Jesus, and God's continued, graceful presence. It mirrors the influence of our beliefs upon our actions. Come now with God's support and sustenance and begin this quiet time.

Collect

We come here, God, to examine the old ways we need to shed as people of faith. You invite us to ponder the difference between what we believe and how we act. Help us grow in truth. Help us determine what is sacrifice and what is for offering in gratitude. For the sake of Christ. Amen.

Prayer Of Confession

Leader: As we begin this searching time of Lent, let us ask whom we are trying to impress.

People: God, let the actions of our regret be private lest they focus attention on us.

Leader: Let us ask how we can best express our trying to be acceptable before God.

All: Let the deepening of our Lenten attitudes and actions toward others reflect a deepening faith. Amen.

19A Hymns[1]

"Before The Cross Of Jesus" Tune: ST. CHRISTOPHER
"Have Thine Own Way, Lord" Tune: ADELAIDE
"Lord, Dismiss Us With [Thy][Your] Blessing" Tune: SICILIAN MARINERS

---

1. At each Lenten worship, sing a verse of "We Are The Cared About People" (Tune: KARED ABOUT) as an introit before the call to worship.

First Sunday In Lent

First Lesson: Genesis 2:15-17; 3:1-7
Theme: Open Your Eyes

Call To Worship

Leader: Open your eyes.

People: Adam and Eve succumbed to temptation. They were human.

Leader: Open your eyes.

People: Jesus withstood temptation. His purpose stretched beyond himself.

Leader: Open your eyes. Be aware of your human nature. Attend to your spiritual nature. Come, let us worship God.

People: We have come to worship God.

Collect

We stand here in the middle of the garden, O God, aware of the chasm between who we are and the person we would be. While it still whispers, teach us to listen to the inner sense of right. When we discover we are naked, let us not run away but sew fig leaves and move beyond innocence toward integrity. Amen.

Prayer Of Confession

As we discover anew that we are vulnerable, human, imperfect beings, guide our growth, O God. As we notice the subtle ways we yield to temptations, draw us away from self-loathing. As we find a little space in our lives for you, restore our conviction that you stand with us through all things. Amen.

20A Hymns[1]

"[God Reigns O'er All The Earth][This Is My Father's World]" Tune: TERRA BEATA

"Open My Eyes, That I May See" Tune: OPEN MY EYES

"[Blessed][Blest] Be The Tie That Binds" Tune: BOYLSTON or DENNIS

First Sunday In Lent

Second Lesson: Romans 5:12-19
Theme: All The Difference

Call To Worship
Adam and Eve pulled us into reality. Adam and Eve pointed to endings but not the end of us. Jesus leads us through the real world. Jesus directs us to new beginnings.

Collect
Though sin and wrong choices are as real today as they became in earliest time, the Son of God has made all the difference. We shall overcome our mistakes because of his compassion and grace. God will see us through. Amen.

Prayer Of Confession
You gave your life, precious Jesus, so we might live finer lives. We will try to do better because of your free gift of forgiveness. We will try to remember beyond Easter. For your sake. Amen.

20A Hymns[1]
"There Is A Green Hill Far Away" Tune: MEDITATION
"It's Me, It's Me, O Lord" Tune: PENITENT
"We Shall Overcome" Tune: WE SHALL OVERCOME

First Sunday In Lent

Gospel: Matthew 4:1-11
Theme: Famished

Call To Worship
We are hungry sojourners on a Lenten journey, pilgrims on a holy trip. Hear God's invitation to make the most of the journey.

Collect
During this Lenten time of reflection, O God, we would work to overcome the temptation to live only for ourselves. Make us increasingly aware of the others who also sojourn in this temporary world. As did Jesus, we can carry one another's load. Amen.

Prayer Of Confession
One thing leads to another, O God, when it comes to temptation. You know our weaknesses, from chocolate to greed, from personal advantage to the urge to cocoon, from compassion exhaustion to just not caring. Come into the midst of our temptations with a nod toward those who suffer. Motion us toward the kind word and the loving act. For the sake of Jesus. Amen.

20A Hymns[1]
"Forty Days And Forty Nights" Tune: HEINLEIN
"We Are Pilgrims On A Holy Trip" Tune: COMPASSION
"Take Time to Be Holy" Tune: HOLINESS or LONGSTAFF

---

1. During Lent, try verse one of "[Behold Us, Lord][O Grant Us, God], A Little Space" (Tune: WINCHESTER OLD) as a response after the confession or before the pastoral prayer.

Second Sunday In Lent

First Lesson: Genesis 12:1-4a
Theme: Obedience

Call To Worship

If Abram could have faith in God, trust God in his heart, and be unafraid — Abram, who was of an older age when God sent him on a journey to leave his own country and go to another land that God was yet to show him — then so might we follow God's call to embark upon a new birth, a journey of faith. Come, for God is calling.

Collect

When you send us on a mission, O God, we also choose to obey you. We will try to be brave and to trust you in our hearts. Amen.

Prayer Of Confession

Leader: I hear God's voice as I deliver Meals On Wheels.
People: I hear God's voice in the harried checkout clerk.
Leader: I hear it in the shabby apartment house downtown,
People: During morning rush in our kitchen,
Leader: At the doctor's office,
People: In an aging parent's phone call,
Leader: In the midst of my own confusion.
All: Here I am. Here I am, let me answer as Jesus would have answered.

21A Hymns

"The Voice Of God Is Calling" Tune: MEIRIONYDD
"I'll Listen To Friends Having Trouble" Tune: PROCRASTINATION
"Have Faith In God, My Heart" Tune: SOUTHWELL

Second Sunday In Lent

Second Lesson: Romans 4:1-5, 13-17
Theme: Believe God

Call To Worship
How easy belief is when little challenges us. How difficult and admirable trust is when things are hard. Come, easy believers and you who struggle with trust. Let us worship God.

Collect
Leader: We turn toward all who would work but cannot.
People: We pray for those caught in company downsizing;
Leader: For those whose disabilities are viewed as inability;
People: For those whose hearts are not in their work.
All: **Teach them to trust, grant them faith and peace.**
Leader: We turn our prayers toward employers.
People: We pray for those who are disillusioned by workers who lack enthusiasm or energy to do the job properly;
Leader: For those who cannot hire the workers they need;
People: For those who must make difficult, even unfair choices in ending an employee's job.
All: **Teach them to trust, grant them faith and peace. Amen.**

Prayer Of Confession
We fret, O God, when we could trust. Talking over our troubles with you does not occur to us. Let us believe that you *are*. Let us trust that we, through you, can believe. Amen.

21A Hymns
"Living With Birthing" Tune: BUNESSAN
"To Christ We Turn" or "Victory In Jesus" Tune: HARTFORD
"Come, Let Us Join With Faithful Souls" Tune: AZMON

Second Sunday In Lent

Gospel: John 3:1-17
Theme: New Birth

Call To Worship

Leader: Hear the call to give your fears to the winds. Hear the call to a new birth, the birth of the spirit.

People: We have come to sing the songs of faith. We gather to sing a new song of hope.

Leader: Come, let us worship God.

Collect

Dear God, open our hearts to hear your voice call in the wind. Let it pipe its tune of spirit through and through our whole being as you deliver renewal of life. Amen.

Prayer Of Confession

We turn things around, O God. We think that we can earn your love by the things we do. Instead, our actions reveal and reflect your love. In the gentleness of your compassion, you so loved the world that you acted, you gave so that we might know love and, in turn, might love others. For this, O Holy, Giving, and Forgiving Parent, we are grateful. Amen.

21A Hymns

"I Am [Yours][Thine], O Lord" Tune: I AM THINE
"Give To The Winds Thy Fears" or "Give Up Your Anxious Pains"
   Tune: ICH HALTE TREULICH STILL or ST. BRIDE
"Come, O Fount Of Every Blessing" Tune: NETTLETON

Third Sunday In Lent

First Lesson: Exodus 17:1-7
Theme: With Us Or Not?

Call To Worship

Two sides comprise every journey: the found side during which we trust in God's care, and the lost side where we fear that alone we will not make it through. At the worst, we scuffle and fuss within the confines of confusion, then shout, "Are you here with us or not, God?" At the best, we quiet down, hear God's voice in the silence, and proceed with hope. Wherever you are on your present journey, know that, here, you are welcome.

Collect

You see through the quarreling within our soul, O God, that we must have the water necessary for life if our journey is to lead to life. Your provision of the water of life assures us that you are here travelling with us. Amen.

Prayer Of Confession

Gracious God, strengthen our capacity to divide the journey into manageable stages so we can escape becoming overwhelmed and afraid that you have deserted us in some wasteland. Amen.

22A Hymns

"When Israel Was In Egypt's Land" Tune: GO DOWN, MOSES
"Nearer, My God, To Thee" Tune: BETHANY
"Lead Us From Death To Life" Tune: WORLD PEACE PRAYER

Third Sunday In Lent

Second Lesson: Romans 5:1-11
Theme: Because Of God

Call To Worship

Leader: Know that our faith frees us. Through Jesus Christ, we find
peace with God. Because of our peace with God and because of God's peace with us, we shall find peace with ourselves.

People: Because of God, we can know peace. Thanks be to God.

Collect

You know where we hurt, O God, and what causes us to be brokenhearted. You know what we can change and over what we have
little power. You know where we are weak, but you see us as worthy
of your compassion. Rather than abandoning us, you bring reconciliation and the amazement of grace. Through Christ. Amen.

Prayer Of Confession

In our yearning for wholeness, O God, we forget to sit still, to turn
toward that quiet center where we begin to listen to you. Hush the
racket of conflict within and around us so that we might reach into the
silence and know your peace. Through Jesus Christ. Amen.

22A Hymns

"A Mighty Fortress Is Our God" Tune: EIN' FESTE BURG
"We Yearn, O [Christ][Lord], For Wholeness" or "O Sacred Head,
Now Wounded" Tune: PASSION CHORALE
"Jesus, Savior, Pilot Me" Tune: PILOT

Third Sunday In Lent

Gospel: John 4:5-42
Theme: Water Of Life

Call To Worship
God is spirit, and those who worship him must worship in spirit and truth. Come, for it is time to worship God.

Collect
So little we know about the eternal, O God. The closest we come is in those moments that seem to transcend time yet somehow also hold the kernel of all time. So little we know about you, Spirit God, still full of mystery, and yet a part of us seems to know you completely. Amen.

Prayer Of Confession
Where do you get that living water, God? What is this thirst that it will quench? Give me a drink, dear God. Amen.

22A Hymns
"Jesus, Keep Me Near The Cross" Tune: NEAR THE CROSS
"We Want To Learn To Live In Love" Tune: CANONBURY
"When Life The Woman At The Well" Tune: CRAVEN

Fourth Sunday In Lent

First Lesson: 1 Samuel 16:1-13
Theme: Looking On The Heart

Call To Worship

Leader: What would happen if we looked not only at the professional stature, economic standing, or physical being of those
we meet?

**People: What would happen if we were to greet others by look-
ing on the heart?**

Leader: If we did not look at the outward appearance, past history,
or patterns of shortcoming?

**People: If we were to weigh the threads of promise beginning to
shape the fabric of a person?**

All: Let us focus on the signs the heart offers.

Collect

We pray, O God, to move away from judging. Let us see our
prejudices in the clarity of light. Let our journey proceed with a spirit
of acceptance and positive regard toward others. Amen.

Prayer Of Confession

Generous God, as we practice the art of generosity, remind us also
to be charitable in spirit toward ourselves. As you respond to us with
compassion, remind us to give ourselves a second chance. Let your
spirit move within us. Amen.

23A Hymns

"Unto The Hills We Lift Our Longing Eyes" Tune: SANDON
"Father, Hear The Prayer We Offer" Tune: REGENSBURG
"Faith Of Our Fathers" Tune: ST. CATHERINE

Fourth Sunday In Lent

Second Lesson: Ephesians 5:8-14
Theme: As Children Of Light

Call To Worship
God calls us to be children of light. Children are active, hopeful, optimistic, and enthusiastic. Undaunted, children try again and again. Children are in touch with what is true, what is fair, and what is good. Let us be children of light.

Collect
In the silence of Lenten darkness, we return to ourselves and find to our surprise that no darkness is completely black. Even there, you are, O God, with a piece of light breaking into the dark. Your light seeps into the dark and soon the light overpowers the dark.

Prayer Of Confession
We would live as children of light, O God of Light, routing out darkness with light. We would be active rather than passive in our faith. With the light God offers, we would expose unfair perspectives, policies, and practices. Strengthen our boldness with your spirit, O God, so we might do what is good, right, and true. In Jesus' name. Amen.

22A Hymns
"When I Survey The Wondrous Cross" Tune: HAMBURG
"In The Silence" Tune: CENACLE
"[O][Our] God, Our Help In Ages Past" Tune: ST. ANNE

Fourth Sunday In Lent

Gospel: John 9:1-41
Theme: Jesus, Light Of The World

Call To Worship
Jesus, your stories and your deeds open the eyes of our heart to the suffering of the world. You unlock the just and the right. You reveal the truth of compassion and the power of love. How fortunate that you have come to live among us, even for so short a time.

Collect
As long as you are in the world, Jesus, you are the light of the world. When you are no longer here, then we must keep the light for you. We will carry the light you have shone for us. For your sake. Amen.

Prayer Of Confession
When our eyes are newly open, O God, we are nearly overcome by what is wrong in the world. We recoil at rampant unfairness. We shrink at the strength of our wrongs. Help us to balance injury with right. Especially while on the Lenten journey, give us the eyes to see possibility. Strengthen our capacity to look and act through eyes of hope. For Jesus' sake. Amen.

23A Hymns
"Tell Me The [Old, Old Story][Stories] Of Jesus" Tune: STORIES OF JESUS
"Precious Lord, Take My Hand" Tune: PRECIOUS LORD
"Pass Me Not, O Gentle Savior" Tune: PASS ME NOT

Fifth Sunday In Lent

First Lesson: Ezekiel 37:1-14
Theme: You Shall Live

Call To Worship

Leader: And God said, "You shall live; and you shall know that I am the Lord." Come, let us surround ourselves with the compassion of God who gathers up our brokenness and binds it with the wholeness of a new vitality.

People: We come with all our brokenness. We come in search of new life. We come to worship our compassionate Creator.

Collect

Did you give us life from a distance, then set us loose, O God? We cannot fathom one so faithfully close as to impart breath to flagging spirits. We want to be in control of our own lives. With a quiet alleluia, let us hear you whisper, "You shall live." Amen.

Prayer Of Confession

We worry about clothing and length of hair, about poundage and heft, and stuff and things — then wonder why our soul is a bag of dry bones. Hearten us, that we might become aware of your spirit within us. Weaken our resistance to accepting your continuous renewal of creation within us. Through Christ. Amen.

24A Hymns

"It Only Takes A Spark" Tune: PASS IT ON
"March On, O Soul, With Strength" Tune: ARTHUR'S SEAT
"Rock Of Ages, Cleft For Me" Tune: TOPLADY

Fifth Sunday In Lent

Second Lesson: Romans 8:6-11
Theme: Spirit Is Life

Call To Worship
As we draw closer to the closing days of Jesus' earthly life, let us remember Paul's words to the Romans: To set the mind on the flesh is death, but to set the mind on the Spirit is life and peace.

Collect
Jesus' death on the cross changes forever how we understand death and life. Thank you, Merciful God, for this gift of your Jesus. Amen.

Prayer Of Confession
Death surrounds us, O God — tragedies of disease and accident, release from bodies too worn out to live, deaths from violence, sometimes funeral after funeral. We shy from death because each dying reminds us of our own. Help us to see that while grief, loss, and endings are part of death's reality, death is not the end of us. Because of Good Friday, let us know the peace of setting our minds on the Spirit dwelling within us. Amen.

24A Hymns
"Wake, My Soul" Tune: HAYDN
"Time Moves Forward On Its Way" Tune: POUCHER
"Holy Spirit, Truth Divine" Tune: MERCY

Fifth Sunday In Lent

Gospel: John 11:1-45
Theme: The Resurrection, The Life

Call To Worship

Jesus said, "I am the resurrection and the life. Those who believe in me, even though they die, will live, and everyone who lives and believes in me will never die. Do you believe this?"

Collect

We believe. We go forth in your name, O God, because we believe that you are the resurrection and the life. Amen.

Prayer Of Confession

Even as Jesus attempted to prepare his disciples for his death through the resurrecting of Lazarus, we also cannot fully understand death until we experience it. How can we explain, O God, that Christ's resurrection is not something to believe with our heads? Rather, belief somehow seizes us. Belief takes hold of us and death's terror loses its power. Amen.

24A Hymns

"O God Of Strength" Tune: WELWYN
"Pass Me Not, O Gentle Savior" Tune: PASS ME NOT
"Forth In [Thy][Your] Name, O Lord, I Go" Tune: DUKE STREET
  or MORNING HYMN

Sunday Of The Passion (Sixth Sunday In Lent)

First Lesson: Isaiah 50:4-9a
Theme: Like Flint

Call To Worship
He, who could tenderly sustain the weary with a word, was about to be clobbered. He knew it. He did not run. He faced it. He turned his own other cheek.

Collect
We stand together with you, O Parent of Jesus, through the unholy events of this holy week. We stand with you as you wait with your own face set like flint as you hear him cry out to you on the cross.

Prayer Of Confession
Oh, Lord Jesus, we would be like you. Teach us that we, too, can be brave because you, O God, also stand here with us, helping and supporting us. Therefore, we will get through whatever it is that we must endure. Amen.

25A Hymns
"All Glory, Laud, And Honor" Tune: ST. THEODULPH
"In Heavenly Love Abiding" Tune: NYLAND
"Lord, I Want To Be A Christian" Tune: I WANT TO BE A CHRISTIAN

Sunday Of The Passion (Sixth Sunday In Lent)

Second Lesson: Philippians 2:5-11
Theme: In Human Form

Call To Worship

People love a parade. Crowds raise the spirits. No one mentions if he who rides the donkey on Palm Sunday is smiling. Does he accept the glory of the hosanna? This one who is transparent knows his purpose. We can only suppose that his eyes are straight with the determination of integrity. Come, walk along the path. Come, enjoy the temporary.

Collect

We who have read the story know what is coming this holy week. We savor this glimpse of triumph. Hoping to deafen our uneasiness, we add our voices to the loud hosannas. Hoping to extend the moment, we pluck a frond of palm, then quietly bow it before the approaching hoofs. We have come to honor you, Jesus. Amen.

Prayer Of Confession

We are told that we are special because we are God's people. Let us neither swagger nor strut with false hosannas but walk through our town with the unassuming certainty that we belong to God. Amen.

25A Hymns

"Hosanna, Loud Hosanna" Tune: ELLACOMBE
"[Go][Journey] To [Dark] Gethsemane" Tune: REDHEAD NO. 76
"Ride On! Ride On In Majesty" Tune: ST. DROSTANE

Sunday Of The Passion (Sixth Sunday In Lent)

Gospel: Matthew 26:14—27:66 or Matthew 27:11-54
Theme: Betrayal

Call To Worship
Leader: What would you give me if...?
People: What would you give me if...?
Leader: Back-stabbing, double-crossing,
People: Double-dealing, duplicity,
Leader: Fraud, trickery,
People: Desertion, abandonment.
Leader: What would you give me if...? Not pretty words. There is no way to remedy betrayal, or is there?

Collect
"Surely not I." "I will never desert you." "I do not know the man." Sold. For thirty pieces of silver. Forgive me, God.

Prayer Of Confession
Our love does grow weak, O God. We would like to confess that we love constantly and deeply. Some people do. For most, however, preoccupation with our own lives intrudes upon our loving. We can be bought. We betray you, God, and we let down those around us. Strengthen our love for you and for others because of Jesus. Amen.

25A Hymns
"Ah, Holy Jesus" Tune: HERZLIEBSTER JESU
"When My Love To God Grows Weak" Tune: SONG 13
"[Go][Journey] To [Dark] Gethsemane" Tune: REDHEAD NO. 76

Holy/Maundy Thursday

First Lesson: Exodus 12:1-4 (5-10) 11-14
Theme: Remembering

Call To Worship

Leader: On Maundy Thursday, we remember God's words to Moses
          at the Passover: "This day shall be a day of remembrance
          for you." We remember Jesus' words as he took the bread
          and the cup after supper in the upper room: "Do this in re-
          membrance of me."
People: Today is a day for remembering.

Collect

We are here to remember you. Instead, you have a way of returning us to ourselves. You remind us we are worth saving. The blood of
the sacrificial lamb signaled your saving the faithful long ago. The
cup of the covenant reminds us of Jesus' sacrifice so we might be
saved. You keep your promises. Amen.

Prayer Of Confession

Gracious God, at times we are so involved with our own problems
that we do not remember your remembering us. Forgive our forgetting that at the Passover you recognized the faithful in each house
marked with blood. Forgive our forgetting that you allowed the sacrifice of your son because we are your remembered people. Amen.

26A Hymns

"Let Us Break Bread Together" Tune: LET US BREAK BREAD
"Jesus Took The Bread" Tune: NEW HOPE
"Just As I Am" Tune: WOODWORTH

Holy/Maundy Thursday

Second Lesson: 1 Corinthians 11:23-26
Theme: Each Time

Call To Worship

Each time we share the elements of Holy Communion, we hand on to someone the truth of Jesus Christ. Each time we share the Lord's Supper, we receive this truth anew. Come to the table with friends.

Collect

We break bread together, O God, for communion is more than a solitary act. We break bread together because of the open arms of the cross that extend to embrace all humankind. We break bread together in the name of Jesus. Amen.

Prayer Of Confession

From Advent through the baptism, the life, and the ministry of Jesus and forward to tomorrow, Easter, and Pentecost — it all comes together here in the upper room at the last supper. Each time we share this holy meal, O God, may we eat it as if it were for the first time at the first supper. Amen.

26A Hymns

"Bread Of The World" Tune: EUCHARISTIC HYMN
"Christ At Table There With Friends" Tune: MAUNDY THURSDAY
"Let Us Break Bread Together" Tune: LET US BREAK BREAD

Holy/Maundy Thursday

Gospel: John 13:1-17, 31b-35
Theme: I Wonder

Call To Worship
"I wonder as I wander out under the sky, how Jesus the Savior was born for to die."

Collect
We can only wonder with awe tonight, Jesus, but you know fully what is about to happen to you. You will teach us right to your earthly end because that is who you are, teacher. You know God's plan for you and for us. But we wonder as we wander, dear Jesus. Amen.

Prayer Of Confession
It seems to take a lifetime of spiritual growing, O God, for us to understand about these things — as you insist on washing our feet even when we resist, even when we are about to betray you and you know it, even when — so we will wash one another's feet and have love for each other. In your name. Amen.

26A Hymns
"Go To Dark Gethsemane" Tune: REDHEAD NO. 76
"I Wonder As I Wander" Tune: I WONDER AS I WANDER
"Out Of The Depths, O God, We Call" Tune: FENNVILLE

Good Friday

First Lesson: Isaiah 52:13—53:12
Theme: Out Of Anguish

Call To Worship
Out of his anguish he shall see light, the writer of Isaiah tells us. Let us embrace these words on this sad day that marks the physical death of Jesus.

Collect
On Good Friday, we see only Good Friday. Give us the grace to remember the Easter light that will come as a result of the anguish of today. Amen.

Prayer Of Confession
We will never understand the "why" of human suffering, O God, only that it is. Draw us toward the truth that out of our distress we will also find a new sense of meaning in the light of Easter. Through Christ. Amen.

27A Hymns
"O Sacred Head, Now Wounded" Tune: PASSION CHORALE
"He Never Said A Mumbalin' Word" Tune: SUFFERER
"Out Of The Depths I Call" Tune: ST. BRIDE

Good Friday

Second Lesson: Hebrews 10:16-25
Theme: Hearts Sprinkled Clean

Call To Worship

Leader: Good Friday is about God's keeping of promises. Come, worship, and witness how on this day God puts God's laws into our hearts.

People: Let us approach God with a true heart in full assurance of faith.

Collect

Because of your actions this day, O God, we are free to go forward in our lives with hearts sprinkled clean from an evil conscience and bodies washed with pure water. O Thou, keeper of promises, we honor and worship you. In Jesus' name. Amen.

Prayer Of Confession

Leader: God, hear the cries of your people.

People: Why must we kill you every year on Good Friday? Is our coming here once in a lifetime not enough? You said Jesus' death was once and for all. Why are we not better people? Why are we so human?

Leader: Forgive us, God, for being so slow to hear you in our hearts. Forgive us, God, for killing you not only on this day but each time we stifle another person with unkindness and each time we set ourselves apart from the new, living way you have opened for us. Through Jesus. Amen.

27A Hymns

"On A Hill Far Away" Tune: THE OLD RUGGED CROSS
"What Wondrous Love Is This" Tune: WONDROUS LOVE
"Were You There?" Tune: WERE YOU THERE

85

Good Friday

Gospel: John 18:1—19:42
Theme: I Am He

Call To Worship
For this Jesus was born, and for this Jesus came into the world: to testify to the truth. Jesus testified to the truth by his words and by his deeds. Ultimately, he proved the truth by offering his body.

Collect
To thank you for giving your life for us, O Christ, we offer our lives in service to others. Amen.

Prayer Of Confession
You did not hesitate, O Christ, to say, "I am he." We would be as brave to stand up for what we believe. We sing Amen and Amen for your life. Soon, when today has passed, we will sing again alleluia to you, our Savior. Amen.

27A Hymns
"Ah, Holy Jesus" Tune: HERZLIEBSTER JESU
"Amen, Amen" Tune: AMEN[1]
"Beneath The Cross Of Jesus" Tune: ST. CHRISTOPHER

---

1. Sing this Epiphany spiritual softly to remind us of the whole story.

Easter (Resurrection Of Our Lord)

First Lesson: Acts 10:34-43
Theme: The Whole Story

Call To Worship

Leader: This is Easter news: Everyone who believes in Jesus Christ receives forgiveness of sins through his name.

People: This is the Easter story.

Leader: Bit by bit and piece by piece, the message enters our hearts anew that Jesus Christ is sovereign over all.

People: This is the Easter story.

Leader: Even the disciples on the Emmaus road needed to hear the story from Jesus at resurrection.

People: Jesus Christ is sovereign.

Leader: Finally, with the giving of his life, the message of our salvation is complete.

People: We hear the Easter story and sing alleluia. Praise be to God this Easter morning.

Collect

Through the saving grace that you bring, O Christ, all Christians everywhere confess and affirm this day that Jesus is Savior. We are your people, O God, chosen to receive forgiveness of our sins. In the name of Jesus the Christ. Amen.

Prayer Of Confession

Gracious, Triumphant God, we will try to extend Easter beyond one holy, family day by reaching toward the promise of your acceptance of us each day. Help us to take you seriously. Guide us as we try to live according to what is right. Amen.

28A Hymns[1]

"On The Day Of Resurrection" Tune: EMMAUS
"Christ Is [Arisen][Risen]" Tune: W ZLOBIE LEZY
"Were You There?" Tune: WERE YOU THERE

Easter (Resurrection Of Our Lord)

Second Lesson: Colossians 3:1-4
Theme: Risen!

Call To Worship

Leader: Today is Easter.
People: Alleluia!
Leader: Christ is risen.
People: Alleluia! Christ is risen.
Leader: Because he lives, we can face tomorrow.
People: Because he lives, we can meet today.
All: Alleluia! Christ is risen.

Collect

Because Christ lives, O God, we can face tomorrow. We can meet uncertainty without feeling abandoned or deserted. Because Christ lives, everything is different for us. We no longer need to worry about our own death because Christ will be with us. What was once fearfully unknown we can greet with hope. Because Christ lives this Easter day, O God, we also are set free. Amen.

Prayer Of Confession

Somehow, O God, the miracle and mystery of this day have managed to reach into our lives. Easter was not only a "back then" event but is for today and for tomorrow. Somehow, O God, the truth that you did this all for our sake has begun to penetrate our hearts. Thank you for Easter morning. Amen.

28A Hymns[1]

"He Lives" Tune: ACKLEY
"In [Thee][You] Is Gladness" Tune: IN DIR IST FREUDE
"God Of The Sparrow, God Of The Whale" Tune: ROEDER **OR** "Because [He Lives][You Live, O Christ]" Tune: RESURRECTION or VRUECHTEN

Easter (Resurrection Of Our Lord)

Gospel: John 20:1-18
Theme: Where Is He?

Call To Worship

Leader: Christ is risen!
People: Christ is risen, indeed!
Leader: Come, let us sing praise to God.
People: We sing alleluia, for Christ is risen today.

Collect

We see that you are risen, O Christ, that you are with us. We see you in the nurses and aids who still go about caring. We see you in corporation officials who seek to keep greed within limits. We see you in shopkeepers who refuse to cheat. We see that you are risen, O Christ, and sing praise to you. Amen.

Prayer Of Confession

All: **Like Mary at the tomb, we ask, "Where is he?" Where is he in our breaking relationships? Where is God within the lives of those struggling with chronic conditions? Where is God in houses where family members no longer relate? Where is God among world leaders whose priorities have overlooked people? Where is God in the sixth grade classroom? Among hospital cooks? In the room of a care center resident?**

Leader: Forgive us, God, for we know now when we ask where you are, that we look with the wrong eyes. Open our eyes of faith to see you at work in all lives. In Jesus' name. Amen.

28A Hymns[1]

"Christ The Lord Is Risen Today" Tune: EASTER HYMN
"Thine Is The Glory" sung with "Sing To The Lord A Triumphant Song"[2] Tune: JUDAS MACCABEUS
"The Strife Is O'er" Tune: VICTORY

---

1. On Easter Day and during the Easter season, sing the refrain to "How Great Thou Art" (Tune: HOW GREAT THOU ART) in closing.

2. Invite the congregation and the choir to alternate singing verses of these two hymns.

Second Sunday Of Easter

First Lesson: Acts 2:14a, 22-32
Theme: But God Is

Call To Worship

Leader: Life accidents, turns of events, chance happenings, and even life according to plans can shake us. Know that with God immediately present for us to call upon, not only can we journey through life spiritually unscathed but we can proceed with hope and with assurance.

All: **Praise to the living God.**

Collect

Gracious God, you bring a song to our lips. You warm our hearts with encouragement to keep trying. You invite us to live fully and with design. We are grateful, O God. Amen.

Prayer Of Confession

We, like David, would see you always before us, O God. We would reserve part of our hearts and minds for attending to your presence in our lives. To You, who are with us, in us, and all around us, we give honor and praise. Amen.

29A Hymns

"God, Whose Love Is Reigning O'er Us" Tune: LAUDA ANIMA
"Praise The Lord, His Glories Show" Tune: LLANFAIR
"Sing Praise To God Who Reigns Above" Tune: MIT FREUDEN ZART

Second Sunday Of Easter

Second Lesson: 1 Peter 1:3-9
Theme: Imperishable Inheritance

Call To Worship
One miracle of Easter is that, while we have not seen Christ, we love him and sense his love for us. An outcome of this faith is an indescribable joy. Such joy does not come from eating comfort food, taking the afternoon off, or engaging in other renewing but fleeting activities. Joy connects us with what lasts forever. Joy flows like new birth into a living hope.

Collect
Although we have not seen you, O God, we love you. We have become aware of your saving love for us through the gift of this inheritance. Through Christ. Amen.

Prayer Of Confession
All: **Despite the many words of Easter, dear God, we still wonder if Easter addresses us.**

Leader: Be assured that the words of Easter are for you.

People: **We are concerned that after several days the joy of the Easter words will fade and we will return to the same humdrum.**

Leader: Be confident that while we all return to everyday activities, we have been saved permanently from the power of evil. The peace of God is with us.

People: **The peace of God goes with us. Thanks be to you, O God, our Savior and Sustainer. Amen.**

29A Hymns
"God Of The Living, In Whose Eyes" Tune: GOTTLOB, ES GEHT
"Jesus, The Very Thought Of You [Thee]" Tune: ST. AGNES
"Peace I Leave With You, My Friends" Tune: PEACE, MY FRIENDS

Second Sunday Of Easter

Gospel: John 20:19-31
Theme: Do You Doubt?

Call To Worship
Do not doubt but believe. Receive the Holy Spirit. Blessed are you who have not seen and yet have come to believe. Peace be with you. Come now, as true worshipers to worship God in spirit and in truth.

Collect
We come here hoping to believe. In spite of ourselves, our wanting the tangible proof, we choose to lay aside doubt. Despite ourselves, we choose to see for a moment with other eyes than those of science and logic. We choose to listen in the silence for a presence that needs no hearing or touch. Help us let go of doubt, O God. Amen.

Prayer Of Confession
"Unless I see for myself, feel with my own fingers, and hear first-hand, I will not believe," we say. Forgive us, God, for being so stubbornly unbelieving. Thank you for understanding our peculiarities. Thank you for providing ways for us to leap to belief so we might know that your peace is with us. Amen.

29A Hymns
"God Himself Is [With Us][Present]" Tune: ARNSBERG or WUNDERBARER KONIG
"For The Beauty Of The Earth" Tune: DIX
"The Day Of Resurrection" Tune: LANCASHIRE

Third Sunday Of Easter

First Lesson: Acts 2:14, 36-41
Theme: The Promise Is For You

Call To Worship
Hear Peter's instructions to the crowds after the resurrection: "Save yourselves from this corrupt generation." We have freedom to manage our lives because of Jesus Christ. Let us rejoice.

Collect
All praise to you, O God, who made Jesus both sovereign and savior. All praise to you, O God, whose promises are for us. Amen.

Prayer Of Confession
Because of Easter, we have the freedom to turn around our lives. Help us to avoid contributing to the decline of life around us — in our community, in our family, and in the quality of our decisions. Guide us as we try to make a difference because of the promises you offer us. Through Christ. Amen.

30A Hymns
"O Jesus, Thou Art Standing" Tune: ST. HILDA
"We Come Unto Our Father's God" Tune: NUN FREUT EUCH
"Father, We Praise Thee" Tune: CHRISTE SANCTORUM

Third Sunday Of Easter

Second Lesson: 1 Peter 1:17-23
Theme: Anew

Call To Worship
Through the living, enduring word of God, we are born anew. This is our charge: to love one another from the heart. Let us worship God who cares for us more than we care about ourselves.

Collect
Guide us, O God, toward loving others in the way that you care about us. As Jesus taught. Amen.

Prayer Of Confession
If we are to love one another deeply from the heart, O Caring God, then we must care for others more than they may love themselves. We would love the child who fails in school, the adult in middle life predicaments, the person exhausted from loneliness. Because we have been born anew through Christ, we can love those who can see no future. Amen.

30A Hymns
"Rejoice, [Ye][You] Pure In Heart" Tune: MARION
"Beautiful [Jesus][Savior]" or "Fairest Lord Jesus" Tune: SCHÖNSTER HERR JESU [ST. ELIZABETH]
"[Jesu][Jesus], Priceless Treasure" Tune: JESU, MEINE FREUDE

Third Sunday Of Easter

Gospel: Luke 24:13-35
Theme: Stay With Us

Call To Worship
We never know whom we will meet along the journey. Let each stranger be our teacher. In turn, let us develop a perception enabling us to become teaching strangers for others. Let our meeting extend beyond perfunctory offers of brief hospitality to include nourishment for the soul. We ask God to be with us as we journey together in worship as God's family.

Collect
Stay with us, Wise One, until we recognize your spirit in each act and attitude of good earth stewardship. Stay with us until we recognize you in the single parent who attempts to do everything. Stay with us until we know you in the elder trying to remain in the family house. Stay with us until we are certain of your presence in all life transitions and can rejoice. Amen.

Prayer Of Confession
Like disciples enclosed in cells of grief, we sometimes reach out to strangers with the plea to "stay with us." Like disciples enveloped in issues of self, we sometimes need to "stay with" others. Show us how to be the stranger who walks in listening friendship beside another and asks the right questions. Amen.

30A Hymns
"From All That Dwell Below The Skies" Tune: OLD HUNDREDTH
"Touch The Earth Lightly" Tune: TENDERNESS **OR** "Let There Be Peace On Earth" Tune: WORLD PEACE
"All Glory Be To God On High" Tune: MIT FREUDEN ZART **OR** "All My Hope [Is Firm][On God Is Founded]" Tune: MICHAEL

Fourth Sunday Of Easter

First Lesson: Acts 2:42-47
Theme: Together

Call To Worship
The core group of early Christians found enough strength, discipline, and community to keep the faith alive. Day by day their efforts made a difference. As we gather, let us acknowledge our shared community of faith. Let us worship God.

Collect
We worship together, O God, because we are a community of faith. As the family of God, we study, share, pray, and eat the common meal. In Christ's name. Amen.

Prayer Of Confession
Whenever we become anxious about the continuing life of this church, O God, remind us that together we can make a difference with our faithfulness, discipline, and strength of community. For the sake of Christ. Amen.

31A Hymns
"God Is My Strong Salvation" Tune: MEIN LEBEN
"Spirit Divine, [Attend][Hear] Our Prayers" Tune: NUN DANKET ALL
"How Lovely [Are Thy Dwellings Fair][Is Your Dwelling]" Tune: BISHOPTHORPE

Fourth Sunday Of Easter

Second Lesson: 1 Peter 2:19-25
Theme: Soul Guardian

Call To Worship
Be aware of Christ's example when you suffer for doing right. Avoid the temptation to return like for like in a world overflowing with abuse and exploitation. Know that Christ is the shepherd and guardian of your soul.

Collect
You, O God, have called us to endure by practicing honesty around dishonest people, speaking kind words where hostile words abound, and living with integrity at all cost. Be the guardian of our promises as Christians. Amen.

Prayer Of Confession
We pray for youths of this community as they develop strength of character. Fortify their goal of becoming the best human beings they can be. Strengthen their will to follow Christ's example in daily decisions, especially when they must take unjust peer pressure. Amen.

31A Hymns
"Tell Me the [Story][Stories] Of Jesus" Tune: STORIES OF JESUS
"I Must Tell Jesus" Tune: ORWIGSBURG
"My Life Flows On In Endless Song" or "How Can I Keep From Singing" Tune: ENDLESS SONG

Fourth Sunday Of Easter

Gospel: John 10:1-10
Theme: Stranger Or Shepherd?

Call To Worship

Leader: Come to worship.
People: We come here as strangers.
Leader: You are welcome. Bring the stranger within yourself.
People: We come here as shepherds.
Leader: You are welcome. Bring the shepherding part of yourself.
Come as the whole person that you are.

Collect

You know who we are. You call us by name. You stand at the gate. You open the door. You go before us and lead us on. We follow you. We recognize your voice. We trust you. We are grateful that your caring is serious. We are thankful that you come as shepherd. Amen.

Prayer Of Confession

In our shepherding roles, O God, let us act with the thoughtfulness of a sensitive dog guide. As it gently leads a blind person down steps, teach us to nudge another's soul, then wait, and tap and wait until each step is negotiated with safety, dignity, and tenderness. In the spirit of Christ. Amen.

31A Hymns

"[Savior][Saviour], Like A Shepherd Lead Us" Tune: BRADBURY
"God Is My Shepherd" Tune: BROTHER JAMES' AIR **OR** "The Lord's My Shepherd" Tune: CRIMOND
"Great Is [Your][Thy] Faithfulness" Tune: FAITHFULNESS

Fifth Sunday Of Easter

First Lesson: Acts 7:55-60
Theme: Valor

Call To Worship
The worst they could do to the apostle Stephen was to kill him, yet he prayed to God not to hold it against them. Can we possibly comprehend the inner strength of Christian martyrs who suffered much to further the faith we also profess?

Collect
Hear our prayers, O God, for those around the world who must suffer in the name of their faith. We pray for their continued valor and courage. We pray also for those who harass and torment them. Amen.

Prayer Of Confession
Gracious God, teach us to stand up for what is right and worthy. Help us to be brave when we are asked to do difficult tasks or are sent on upsetting missions. Guide us so we will know what merits sacrifice. In the name of Christ. Amen.

32A Hymns
"Faith Of [Our Fathers][The Martyrs]" Tune: ST. CATHERINE
"Bless [God][The Lord], O My Soul" Tune: SPRING WOODS
"For The Brave Of Every Race" Tune: SALZBURG **OR** "When Stephen, Full Of Power And Grace" Tune: WELLINGTON SQUARE

Fifth Sunday Of Easter

Second Lesson: 1 Peter 2:2-10
Theme: Cornerstones

Call To Worship
Leader: Come, people of God. Come, you who are precious to God. Come, you who have received mercy. Be glad that God is good. Know that you are welcome here in the name of God, our foundation and cornerstone.
People: We come with certainty, confidence, and hope.
All: Praise to Christ, cornerstone of our faith.

Collect
We would return to the infrastructure of our faith. We would remember the cement that hope and trust in you provides. Let us be as earnest in our building of faith foundations as we are in grounding our life work. In Christ's name. Amen.

Prayer Of Confession
When our lives lack design, we stumble around in darkness. Once our foundations are firm, chosen stones become safe, identifiable markers. Lead us, Holy Parent, to recognize these foundation stones with a tap of the toe and to know the serenity of finding home. Amen.

32A Hymns
"We Would Be Building" Tune: FINLANDIA
"God, Creation's Great Designer" Tune: NEW REFORMATION
"Christ Is Made The Sure Foundation" Tune: REGENT SQUARE

Fifth Sunday Of Easter

Gospel: John 14:1-14
Theme: Don't Be Troubled

Call To Worship

"Do not let your hearts be troubled. Believe in God, believe also in me. In my Father's house there are many dwelling places. If it were not so, would I have told you that I go to prepare a place for you? And if I go and prepare a place for you, I will come again and will take you to myself, so that where I am, there you may be also." In a world filled with deception, misguided goals, and wrong motives, we still can trust these comforting words. Praise be to God.

Collect

You sent Jesus the Christ to show us the way, the truth, and the life. When our trust falters, you offer the example of Jesus' works, his words, and his life. Always, O God, you send us your comfort and quiet assurance, and we are grateful. Amen.

Prayer Of Confession

With your comforting words, O God, you anticipate our fears of the unknown. You show us the way through Jesus the Christ who is also the truth and the life. Strengthen our determination to study the words, the work, and the life of Jesus so we might come confidently to you through him. Amen.

32A Hymns

"Come, My Way, My Truth, My Life" Tune: THE CALL
"Thou Hidden Source Of Calm Repose" or "I Sing The Praise Of Love Almighty" Tune: ST. PETERSBURG
"Not As The World Gives, Do You Give" Tune: TOULON or ELLERS

Sixth Sunday Of Easter

First Lesson: Acts 17:22-31
Theme: To A Known God

Call To Worship

Leader: God is a known God who continually gives us evidence of
presence.

**People: God is a knowable God who extends to us the hand of
hope.**

All: Come, let us worship God. Amen.

Collect

In the dauntless first spring flowering of snowdrop and crocus,
you have shown yourself. We see you in the will of a toddler's steps.
In the strength of those with chronic conditions to override the death
wish, you are there. You stand beside persistent peacemakers. You
offer year-end perspective to the schoolteacher. All around us speaks
the voice of a known God. Thanks be to God. Amen.

Prayer Of Confession

We see dimly into the mirror, supposing, O God, that in your su-
premacy you are also unknowable and unapproachable. Yet you show
yourself by the moment to be available at a whisper even in that in-
stant before we become aware of calling to you. Thank you for making yourself known to us. Through Christ. Amen.

33A Hymns

"Blessed Assurance" Tune: ASSURANCE
"Nearer, My God, To Thee" Tune: BETHANY
"[I Sing The Mighty][We Sing The Almighty] Power Of God" Tune:
ELLACOMBE

Sixth Sunday Of Easter

Second Lesson: 1 Peter 3:13-22
Theme: Gentle Hope

Call To Worship
Hope comes slipping in with the tenacity of a too early born infant who is ready to live. Sometimes hope is boisterous; mostly hope is quiet, a nearly touchable presence. Hope expects. Hope is a gift of the spirit.

Collect
As you brought us hope through the life, death, and resurrection of Jesus Christ, O God, may we through our living bring an air of hope to those around us. Amen.

Prayer Of Confession
Teach us to trust that hope is connected to the holy. Teach us to trust that hope is as patient as God. Teach us to trust in hope. In the name of Jesus the Christ. Amen.

33A Hymns
"O Lord And Master Of Us All" Tune: WALSALL
"Be Still And Know That I Am God" Tune: MAPLE
"We Can Be Hope" Tune: OHIO

Sixth Sunday Of Easter

Gospel: John 14:15-21
Theme: I Will Not Leave You Orphaned

Call To Worship

Leader: God will not leave you orphaned.
People: Among our greatest fears is being abandoned.
Leader: God is coming to you.
People: We do not want to be deserted.
Leader: God will give you another advocate to be with you forever.
This is the Spirit of truth within you.

Collect

Spirit of truth, be with us always. In return, because of our love for you, we will keep your commandments. Because Christ lives in Spirit, we also live. Thanks be to God. Amen.

Prayer Of Confession

We call it intuition, conscience, scruples, or wisdom. We call it good upbringing, principles, or morals. Maybe all the time it has been you, God, finding one more way to make yourself known to us. Spirit of truth, be our champion. Whisper into our hearts the work of the Holy Spirit. Amen.

33A Hymns

"O Gracious God, Whose Constant Care" Tune: LOBT GOTT IHR CHRISTEN
"Be Not Dismayed" or "God Will Take Care Of You" Tune: MARTIN
"Joys Are Flowing Like A River" Tune: BLESSED QUIETNESS

Ascension Of Our Lord

First Lesson: Acts 1:1-11
Theme: Sonlight

Call To Worship

Leader: We have only begun to recognize God as Creator and Sustainer. We have only started to grasp the strength of the Holy Spirit. Come, let us explore the light of the Son.

People: At ascension, we sense Christ's reality beyond historical boundaries. God has not moved out of our grasp but has expanded to include everyone's reach. Amen.

Collect

Like the disciples at Christ's ascension, O God, we fear that you are beyond us. Each time we release ideas too small to contain you, we also step into new territory. As Christ raised his hands in blessing to receive whatever was coming, so we pray to know a similar openness of spirit and attitude. Amen.

Prayer Of Confession

Instead of shrugging shoulders in confusion, let us lift up our arms in expectant blessing. We ask for the courage to greet continual changes in life with an acceptance that transcends resignation and with a sense of adventure that overrides apprehension. Amen.

34A Hymns

"All Creatures Of Our God And King" Tune: LASST UNS ERFREUEN

"O Grant Us Light" Tune: HESPERUS **OR** "Let There Be Light, Lord God Of Hosts" Tune: ELTON or PENTECOST

"All Hail The Power Of Jesus' Name" Tune: CORONATION or MILES LANE

Ascension Of Our Lord

Second Lesson: Ephesians 1:15-23
Theme: Spirit Of Wisdom And Revelation

Call To Worship
Ascension is a time for giving encouragement. Christ had shown himself to the disciples after the resurrection. The finality of witnessing his rising out of sight required great faith from the disciples. For us, ascension is a time of piecing together our quilt of faith.

Collect
We remember in prayer all who try to make sense out of the events from Easter to Pentecost. Help us to grow in faith. Help us, through the Holy Spirit, to thrive with wisdom and understanding. Amen.

Prayer Of Confession
Help us to remember, O God, that faith is a lifelong process. Our faith matures as we practice having hope. Our faith increases as we come to know you with the eyes of our heart enlightened by the working of your power. Through the Holy Spirit. Amen.

34A Hymns
"At The Name Of Jesus" Tune: KING'S WESTON
"We Live By Faith And Not By Sight" Tune: DUNLAP'S CREEK
"Praise To The Lord, The Almighty" or "Sing Praise To God" Tune:
LOBE DEN HERREN

Ascension Of Our Lord

Gospel: Luke 24:44-53
Theme: Huddle

Call To Worship

There is a time to rush out and spread the news. There is a time to huddle. Before blessing the disciples prior to his ascension, Jesus instructed them to stay in the city until they received God's power. Our time together in worship is a time to huddle, to conference and to consult, and to prepare for the next action of faith.

Collect

As you opened the minds of the disciples to understand the scriptures, open our minds, O God, to receive insight and understanding before jumping into action without the guidance of the Spirit. Amen.

Prayer Of Confession

Teach us to have patience with the process of huddling, O God. Strengthen us to wait before going out to serve you ill-equipped or single-handed. Nurture a sense of sustaining community within our congregation. Through your Spirit. Amen.

34A Hymns

"Christ Is The World's Light" Tune: CHRISTE SANCTORUM **OR** "Christ Is The World's True Light" Tune: O GOTT, DU FROMMER GOTT

"Surely Goodness And Mercy Shall Follow You" Tune: SURELY GOODNESS AND MERCY

"Jesus Shall Reign" Tune: DUKE STREET

Seventh Sunday Of Easter

First Lesson: Acts 1:6-14
Theme: Angels?

Call To Worship

Even the disciples needed an emissary in the time between the ascension and the Holy Spirit's coming. They asked questions of Jesus until the last moment. Let us be aware of the intermediaries God also sends for our support.

Collect

We bring our trust to you, O God, especially when we are filled with doubt and puzzling. We listen for any hints of direction for our lives that you choose to impart. With the hope of Christ. Amen.

Prayer Of Confession

Like the disciples' need for an emissary, we too would rather ask until the last moment the questions that mark our insecurity. At the right time, guide us away from pondering distress and toward the action that faith engenders. Amen.

35A Hymns

"[Ye][You] Servants Of God" Tune: HANOVER
"Be [Now][Thou] My Vision" Tune: SLANE
"Have Faith In God, My Heart" Tune: SOUTHWELL

Seventh Sunday Of Easter

Second Lesson: 1 Peter 4:12-14; 5:6-11
Theme: God Of Grace

Call To Worship

Cast all your anxiety on God, the writer says. Don't just stand quietly before God with your woes. Get rid of them. Put some energy into it like the fishers of Jesus' day who hurled their nets into the sea. Come deliberately to God with your troubles, because our God of grace cares enough for you to receive your anxiety and thereby to relieve it.

Collect

Who is this God who accompanies us through all ordeals? The God of all grace who has called us to God's eternal glory in Christ, who will restore, support, strengthen, and establish us. Praise be to God. Amen.

Prayer Of Confession

When we are troubled, our anxieties circle around and around inside us like a thunderstorm squalling into the night. Keep us in touch with you during these times, Compassionate Sustainer, so we will remember you and come to you with our burdens. In the name of Christ. Amen.

35A Hymns

"Blessed Jesus, At Thy Word" Tune: LIEBSTER JESU
"Give To The Winds Thy Fears" or "Give Up Your Anxious Pains"
    Tune: ICH HALTE TREULICH STILL or ST. BRIDE
"Love Divine, All Loves Excelling" Tune: BEECHER or HYFRYDOL

Seventh Sunday Of Easter

Gospel: John 17:1-11
Theme: Heart Talk

Call To Worship

Leader: We come to this place to speak heart to heart with God. We can tell God what is on our minds and in our hearts.

People: We come to this place because we know Whose we are. Come, let us worship the God of all people in all time and in every place.

Collect

We come to you, all-encompassing God, with the assurance that you hear and care about what we have to say. Jesus turned us over to you with the same affection and concern with which he put his disciples into your care. We are yours forever. Amen.

Confession

At times, God, we lose inner sight of to Whom we belong. We forget who we are and wander about lost. Help us when we stand in need of prayer, O God, to make a little space for returning things to order. Guide us toward the right thinking that all people on earth dwell secure within your protective care. Amen.

35A Hymns

"Immortal, Invisible, God Only Wise" Tune: ST. DENIO
"[O Grant Us, God][Behold Us Lord], A Little Space" Tune: WIN-CHESTER OLD **OR** "It's Me, O Lord" Tune: PENITENT
"All People That On Earth Do Dwell" Tune: OLD HUNDREDTH

The Day Of Pentecost

First Lesson: Acts 2:1-21
Theme: I Hear!

Call To Worship

Leader: Can you hear the Spirit of God when the wind whispers? When it blusters? What sort of wind do you need for God to gain your attention? In order to comprehend God's reality? What language reaches your heart?

People: If we are to communicate as Christians, first we must hear the Spirit of God. We trust the Holy Spirit to blow without understanding from where it comes or to where it blows.

All: Like wind across the plain — silent until it flutes past our ears, transparent until it presses against us — your Spirit shows itself, O Sustainer. Amen.

Collect

We see from Pentecost, O God, that you want to connect with us. Sharpen our souls to hear you. Quicken our awareness of the softest breeze of your spirit. Through the risen Christ. Amen.

Prayer Of Confession

Quiet the inner babble that prevents us from hearing the language of others. Attune the song of our soul to harmonize with your song, Savior God. Amen.

36A Hymns[1]

"This Is The Day" Tune: THIS IS THE DAY **OR** "Crown [Him] With [Your Richest][Many] Crowns" Tune: DIADEMATA

"Come, O Spirit, Dwell Among Us" or "God Hath Spoken By The Prophets" Tune: EBENEZER

"Holy Spirit, Truth Divine" Tune: MERCY

The Day Of Pentecost

Second Lesson: 1 Corinthians 12:3-13
Theme: Spice Of Life

Call To Worship
Look around you at this unique collection of faces. With a variety of talents also, God has created a diverse, fascinating world. Together as the family of God, we share many ways of serving God with our gifts. Let us worship the Creator.

Collect
Creator God, we marvel at your imagination. You must enjoy the promise of human creation. Our prayer is to so live that we will fulfill your plans for us and to bring you enjoyment. As we are all one in the Holy Spirit. Amen.

Prayer Of Confession
Let us be mindful of the particular gift of the Holy Spirit which you have chosen for each of us, O God. Let us do well to nurture, prepare, and use that gift to bring you honor and, subsequently, to know joy in ourselves and in others. Amen.

36A Hymns[1]
"Forward Through The Ages" Tune: ST. GERTRUDE
"Send Down Thy Truth, O God" Tune: ST. MICHAEL
"They'll Know We Are Christians By Our Love" Tune: ST. BRENDAN'S **OR** "God Of Change And Glory" Tune: KATHERINE

The Day Of Pentecost

Gospel: John 7:37-39
Theme: Pentecost

Call To Worship
As winds of the atmosphere signify a change of weather, so does the wind at Pentecost carry a change in our concept of God. Come, let us worship the triune God.

Collect
At this time long ago, Pentecost marked the end of the harvest season by sharing the first fruits with you, O God of creation. So appropriately, O God, you chose this time of special awareness of life's holiness to share yourself as the Holy Spirit. We are grateful, O God. Amen.

Prayer Of Confession
Let us open our hearts as believers ready to receive your Spirit, O Giving God. As receivers of the Holy Spirit, let our way of living in the Spirit know change. Amen.

36A Hymns[1]
"Let Every Christian Pray" Tune: LAUDES DOMINI
"Breathe On Me, Breath Of God" Tune: TRENTHAM
"Gracious Spirit, Dwell With Me" Tune: REDHEAD NO. 76

---

1. For several Sundays in Pentecost, try the second verse of "Take Up The Song" (Tune: ELLERS) as a benediction response.

113

The Holy Trinity

First Lesson: Genesis 1:1—2:4a
Theme: Trinity — In The Beginning

Call To Worship

Leader: In the beginning,
People: God was.
Leader: In our new beginnings,
People: God is.
All: In all beginnings, forever, God is.

Collect

God of all creation, we marvel at your capacity to create and re-create. We stand in awe at the evidence of your obvious perennial caring for your whole world. How wonderful that each human creature is a unique part of your creative expression. We praise you and celebrate your creation. Amen.

Prayer Of Confession

Creator God, we are aware of the two sides of beginnings. On the one hand, we are afraid of beginnings, God, because they are new. Beginnings change us. We forget about courage. We forget to believe. We would rather stay inside the known womb of certainty. On the other hand, we revel in the refreshing creativity of the new. The start of a day offers the grace of beginning again after leaving behind the worn-out ideas and musty ways of doing things. Renew our courage, our sense of celebration, and our joy. Amen.

37A Hymns

"Morning Has Broken" with "Living With Birthing" Tune: BUNESSAN[1]

"Creation's Lord, We Give Thee Thanks" Tune: RAMWOLD **OR** "Creator God, Creating Still" Tune: ST. ANNE

"Holy, Holy, Holy" Tune: NICAEA

---

1. Start with "Morning Has Broken," choir/congregation alternating with verses of "Living With Birthing," ending with first verse again of "Morning."

The Holy Trinity

Second Lesson: 2 Corinthians 13:11-13
Theme: Trinity — Goodbye

Call To Worship
Are your last words as you go out the door also lasting words? We have probably all played the "if you could only take three items with you" game. What last words would you say to people who are important to you? Here are the Apostle Paul's last words to the Corinthians: Put things in order, listen to my appeal, agree with one another, live in peace; and the God of love and peace will be with you. Greet one another with a holy kiss. What memorable words would you offer?

Collect
Gracious God of farewells as well as hellos, you teach us how to say goodbye. You remind us this Trinity Sunday of how the forms in life change — you from Creator to Savior to Sustaining Holy Spirit — yet the essence remains the same. Thank you, O Compassionate One, for understanding our need to know your eternal presence. Amen.

Prayer Of Confession
We bark out last minute laundry lists to college graduates, to kids off to summer play, to relatives leaving on trips. The list lengthens as we wave. Long after they are out of sight, our thoughts follow them with additions now stretching into other things we have always wanted to tell them. It is hard to say goodbye, God, hard to let them go, hard to believe they have compiled their own solid, sensible, sensitive lists. How did you ever let Jesus go, God? Teach us how to say goodbye. Amen.

37A Hymns
"All Glory Be To God On High" Tune: ALLEIN GOTT IN DER HÖH
"Children Of The Heavenly Father" or "Surely No One Can Be Safer"
    Tune: TRYGGARE KAN INGEN VARA
"O God, Thou Art The Father" Tune: DURROW

The Holy Trinity

Gospel: Matthew 28:16-20
Theme: Trinity — Always

Call To Worship
Leader: Hear and carry with you these words: And remember, I am with you always, to the end of the age.
People: Whatever our assignment — activity or inactivity,
Leader: Jesus said, "I am with you always."
People: Whatever our responsibility — invigorating, overwhelming, or disappointing,
Leader: Jesus said, "I am with you always, to the end of the age."

Collect
We hear an inner song, O God, a song of comfort, a song of encouragement, a song of "I am with you always." Thank you. Amen.

Prayer Of Confession
Like summer dismissal of school, when the urge toward irresponsibility rampages through our homes, we hear your nudge as well as your comfort, "I am with you always." As we abandon wintertime activities, remind us that you, O God, take no leave of us these days. Because of Christ. Amen.

37A Hymns
"Come, Holy Spirit, Heavenly Dove" Tune: ST. AGNES
"O Holy God, Whose Gracious Power Redeems Us" Tune: WELWYN
"In My Heart There Rings A Melody" or "There's Within My Heart A Melody" Tune: SWEETEST NAME

Corpus Christi

First Lesson: Deuteronomy 8:2-3, 14-16
Theme: By God's Design

Call To Worship

When the devil tempted Jesus to make bread from stone, Jesus quoted the Deuteronomist: "One does not live by bread alone, but by every word that comes from the mouth of the Lord." The bread that fills the belly and fuels the body is necessary for physical life. The bread which God offers with every word feeds our spirit and is necessary for spiritual life. Come, let us hear the words of God.

Collect

We come before you in humility, Holy God. We remember the stories of manna long ago. We are aware of recent stories of being fed in body and spirit as we journey through the wildernesses of today. We bow before you in gratitude for this nourishment. Amen.

Prayer Of Confession

From the beginning of our religious heritage, Merciful God, we have called to you in the distress of hunger. You have led us through the wilderness. You feed us bread for life and nourishment for eternal life. Teach us to remember that, always, you have a gracious and redeeming plan to do us good. Amen.

38A Hymns

"All People That On Earth Do Dwell" Tune: OLD HUNDREDTH
"Lord, I Want To Be A Christian" Tune: I WANT TO BE A CHRISTIAN
"Through All The Changing Scenes" Tune: WILTSHIRE

117

Corpus Christi

Second Lesson: 1 Corinthians 10:16-17
Theme: Body Of Christ

Call To Worship
Leader: Because there is one bread, we who are many are one body, for we all share the one bread.
People: One bread and one body.
Leader: Come, let us worship God and participate in the holy feast of the blessed sacrament.

Collect
We are one in the spirit, O Holy Father, and in the blood which Christ shares in the cup. We stand in unity because of the body which Christ gives in the bread. Bless today the unity of all around the world who drink and eat of this meal. We ask in the name of Jesus Christ. Amen.

Prayer Of Confession
Holy God, as we ponder the extent of Jesus' sacrifice for us, let us also consider the depth of our commitment to you. Hear our aim to honor Jesus as we try to live in healthy unity with others. Help us to stand true to our promises. We pray through Jesus Christ. Amen.

38A Hymns
"Lord Of The Dance" Tune: LORD OF THE DANCE
"Jesus, [Thou][The] Joy Of Loving Hearts" Tune: HESPERUS
"Lord Of All Hopefulness" Tune: SLANE

Corpus Christi

Gospel: John 6:51-58
Theme: Unless

Call To Worship

Unless we eat of the flesh of the Son of Man and drink his blood, we have no life in us. His flesh is the true food and his blood is the true drink, nourishment for life eternal. Let us worship God.

Collect

How close to us you are, O Living God, in this living and holy meal. We who eat of the elements abide in you and you remain in us. Hear our gratitude for the possibility of such oneness in Christ who shares with us because of his union with you. We pray, therefore, in the name of Jesus Christ. Amen.

Prayer Of Confession

Forgive us, Merciful Creator, when we live in ways that make us unworthy to eat at this holy table. Help us to live lives that reflect unity with all of our brothers and sisters. For the sake of Christ. Amen.

38A Hymns

"Here, O My Lord, I See [Thee][You] Face To Face" Tune: ADORO
   TE
"Break Thou The Bread Of Life" Tune: BREAD OF LIFE
"Bread Of The World" Tune: EUCHARISTIC HYMN

Proper 4
Sunday between May 29 and June 4 inclusive

First Lesson: Genesis 6:11-12; 7:24; 8:14-19
Theme: Arks Of Faith

Call To Worship
God shows interest in every detail. God wanted the ark that safeguarded his creation to be right. Representatives of all God's creatures were on that ark. God's will is for survival. Thanks be to God.

Collect
You said, O God, each day that your creation was good. Thank you for discerning continued worth and possibility in your creation, for seeing us through all assortments of calamity. We praise you for your endless creativity. Amen.

Prayer Of Confession
You have taught us, steadfast Creator, how to build arks of faith. You show us your infinite care with careful instructions. You show us that the survival of faith is not automatic but requires planning, nurture, and dedication. Lead us, O God, toward taking an ever deepening sense of ownership as we do our part to keep alive the important covenants between you and humankind. Amen.

39A Hymns
"O Zion, Haste, Thy Mission High Fulfilling" Tune: TIDINGS
"O Love That [Will][Wilt] Not Let Me Go" Tune: ST. MARGARET
"God Reigns O'er All The Earth" or "This Is My Father's World"
   Tune: TERRA BEATA

Proper 4
Sunday between May 29 and June 4 inclusive

Second Lesson: Romans 1:16-17; 3:22b-28 (29-31)
Theme: The Law Of Faith

Call To Worship

Leader: The power of God is for salvation to everyone who has faith, to the divorced parent, couples with struggling relationships, the almost retirees trying to hold on, the teenager wondering about the future, persons with unusual or alternative lifestyles, those searching for meaning.

People: God's power for salvation is for everyone who has faith.

Leader: God calls us to have faith. Come, worship, be reassured along your journey, and know a strengthening of your faith.

Collect

Gracious, all-powerful God, who cares enough for us to have a plan for our future and a design for our lives, hear the quiet movement of our hearts toward faith. In the name of Jesus the Christ. Amen.

Prayer Of Confession

All: We worry that God will abandon us because we fall short of our expectations and of God's expectations of us. Our lives are filled with the violence of killing thoughts, self-defeating attitudes, and faithless actions. Our ways are corrupt. We stray from our ideals or set ideals so high we do not attempt to meet them. Teach us how to build arks of faith.

Leader: All have sinned and all do not deserve God's praise. Still, we are now justified by God's grace as a gift because of what happened on the cross. So have faith and be faithful.

All: Amen.

39A Hymns

"O Jesus, I Have Promised" Tune: ANGEL'S STORY
"I Would Be True" [3 verses in NCH] or [2 verses in PH] Tune: PEEK
"Children Of God" **OR** "O Brother Man, Fold To Thy Heart" Tune:
   WELWYN or INTERCESSOR

Proper 4
Sunday between May 29 and June 4 inclusive

Gospel: Matthew 7:21-29
Theme: Rock Solid

Call To Worship
The most beautiful sanctuary will crumble if built on prestige, self-indulgence, or wrong reasons. Come, people of God, come to church for the right reasons. Be God's steady and steadfast church.

Collect
We are here, O God, to learn about your will for us and for this church. May your will be done. May this church stay as solid as the rock upon which it was founded. In the name of Christ. Amen.

Prayer Of Confession
We go off on our own tangents when what we need to do is return to you, O God. Help us to quiet our agendas so we can listen to your words and hear them with enough clarity to act wisely on them. Reassure us that, while temporary distresses threaten, they can not ultimately destroy what is firm. Amen.

39A Hymns
"Built On The Rock The Church Doth Stand" Tune: KIRKEN DEN ER ET
"O Master Workman Of The Race" Tune: KINGSFOLD
"O Word Of God Incarnate" Tune: MUNICH

Proper 5
Sunday between June 5 and June 11 inclusive

First Lesson: Genesis 12:1-9
Theme: Go, Come, Be A Blessing

Call To Worship

Leader: Go!
People: Come!
All: Be a blessing!
Leader: We hear the word "blessing," and know it as a special word
for someone else, certainly not for us. Then a person whom
we respect tells us, "You are a blessing," and we ponder
those words. Turn now to someone near you. Quietly say
to each other, "You are a blessing." During this time of
worship consider how, indeed, you are a blessing.

Collect

Go, be a blessing, you told Abram, O God of blessings. Go, be a
blessing to others, you tell us, because you are a blessing to me, your
God. Open our hearts, dear God, to hear your affirming "I Am" about
ourselves. Let us nod and smile and agree that we are worthy of your
love and your blessing. Let us go and be a blessing because you have
blessed our being from the beginning. Amen.

Prayer Of Confession

Embarrassed? Yes, a little, God. Mostly, we think about the ways
we are not a blessing to others, to ourselves, and to you. Forgive us
when we focus on things that bring the death of our soul instead of
drawing us toward a life that gently blesses. Amen.

40A Hymns

"Spirit, Spirit Of Gentleness" Tune: SPIRIT
"Spirit Of The Living God" Tune: IVERSON
"Guide Me, O [My Great Redeemer][Thou Great Jehovah]" Tune:
CWM RHONDDA

Proper 5
Sunday between June 5 and June 11 inclusive

Second Lesson: Romans 4:13-25
Theme: Buoyancy

Call To Worship

Leader: How do we grow strong in our faith?
People: First, give God some credit.
Leader: Be convinced that God is able to do as God has promised.
People: Practice being faithful.
Leader: Avoid weakening when we observe what is already weak.
People: Adopt an attitude of faith.
Leader: Choose hope, where there is little hope.
People: Believe that what you hope for will happen.

Collect

When our faith quivers, we remember the miracle that faith is and look up to you, O Faithful One. Amen.

Prayer Of Confession

The same water that could drown us, dear God, cradles us in an easy float when we trust it and skim across the pool. We could follow the rules of a swim stroke, proper kick, and regulation of breathing, yet still sink to the bottom if we did not first trust the water. Give us the courage to love you with that faith, Thou Great Sustainer. As Jesus taught us. Amen.

40A Hymns

"He Lives" Tune: ACKLEY
"My Faith Looks Up to Thee" Tune: OLIVET
"Who Trusts In God, A Strong Abode" Tune: WAS MEIN GOTT WILL

Proper 5
Sunday between June 5 and June 11 inclusive

Gospel: Matthew 9:9-13, 18-26
Theme: Mercy

Call To Worship
Leader: When we sacrifice, we have something to offer. We give up something that we cherish. With sacrifice, we have the possibility and power of choice. Sacrifice is a gift to others.
People: Mercy meets our posture of vulnerability. Mercy asks us to receive compassion, forgiveness, and kindness as a path to wholeness. Mercy is a gift to us.
All: Praise to our healing God.

Collect
We honor you, O Christ, who dares to enter places we would rather not go. We honor you, O Christ, whose awareness knows who is broken. We honor you, O Christ, worker of miracles. Amen.

Prayer Of Confession
It is easier for us to mingle with the righteous than to seek out the troubled. We fancy ourselves to be righteous while trying to ignore that we, too, need healing. We, too, need to ask mercy of you. Amen.

40A Hymns
"Immortal Love, Forever Full" or "Serenity" Tune: BEATITUDO or SERENITY
"O Christ, The Healer, We Have Come" Tune: KENTRIDGE **OR** "Heal Me, Hands Of Jesus" Tune: SUTTON COMMON
"Savior, Again To [Thy][Your] Dear Name" Tune: ELLERS

Proper 6
Sunday between June 12 and June 18 inclusive

First Lesson: Genesis 18:1-15
Theme: Hospitable

Call To Worship
Like Abraham's greeting to strangers by the oaks of Mamre, come to worship today with a renewing spirit of hospitality — hospitality toward the stranger who brings a message, hospitality toward a baby given and growing within, receptivity toward what seems impossible, openness toward a new idea. Offer a little water, select the choice flour and a tender, good calf. Refresh soul and body and prepare to listen.

Collect
Like the beauty of a well-seasoned Sarah, we rejoice in the ability to summon our sense of humor, O God. From our depths and even off the top comes miraculous and sustaining resilience. Let us be ready, God, when your hope comes slipping in. Amen.

Prayer Of Confession
Even at tender ages, we sometimes get to thinking, dear God, that we are old, that it is too late for us, that the world is passing us by. Then you surprise us. Let our opening to your surprises carry the relaxed welcome of laughter. Rather than the sneer of incredulity, help us lean toward choosing the laughter that accompanies joy. In the name of Christ. Amen.

41A Hymns[1]
"Hope Of The World" Tune: ANCIENT OF DAYS, DONNE SECOURS, or VICAR

"Let Us Hope When Hope Seems Hopeless" Tune: LET US HOPE or HYFRYDOL

"There's A Wideness In God's Mercy" Tune: IN BABILONE or WELLESLEY

Proper 6
Sunday between June 12 and June 18 inclusive

Second Lesson: Romans 5:1-8
Theme: Hope

Call To Worship
Leader: Suffering produces endurance,
Men: And endurance produces character,
Women: And character produces hope,
All: And hope does not disappoint us, because God's love has been poured into our hearts through the Holy Spirit that has been given to us.

Collect
We are grateful, O God, for the strength of your presence which enables us to move through suffering and to come out on the other side. We come to the comfort of prayer, O Compassionate Creator, because we find peace with you through Jesus Christ. Amen.

Prayer Of Confession
We speak not often about our suffering, dear God, because we try not to dwell on it. In truth, when we hear that suffering produces endurance, we would rather not have the suffering in the first place. Then we see how we have grown through our pain and distress. It is possible to know hope and peace while living with suffering. Thank you, Holy Comforter. Amen.

41A Hymns[1]
"I've Got Peace Like A River" Tune: PEACE LIKE A RIVER
"Come, Ye Disconsolate" Tune: CONSOLATOR
"Near To The Heart Of God" Tune: McAFEE

Proper 6
Sunday between June 12 and June 18 inclusive

Gospel: Matthew 9:35—10:8 (9-23)
Theme: For God

Call To Worship

Leader: These are the twelve disciples Jesus sent out:
Women: Simon Peter and his brother Andrew,
Men: James son of Zebedee, and his brother John,
Women: Philip and Bartholomew,
Men: Thomas and Matthew the tax collector,
Leader: James son of Alphaeus, and Thaddaeus,
Men: Simon the Cananaean, and Judas Iscariot, the one who betrayed Jesus.
Leader: Jesus sent the first disciples to seek out the lost sheep of Israel and to help with his work of healing and proclaiming the good news. He said the work would not be easy.

Collect

We pray for the disciples of yesterday and of today who heard and hear Christ asking if we are able and if we would be willing to do God's work. Help us, today, to give the right answer. In Jesus' name. Amen.

Prayer Of Confession

We ask, O God, for the courage to go forth for you into the world we know. In our own ways, help us to spread the healing that comes with compassion. Help us remember that your grace goes with us and your Spirit speaks through us. In Jesus' name. Amen.

41A Hymns[1]

"Are Ye Able" Tune: BEACON HILL
"God Our Author And Creator" Tune: JEFFERSON
"Go Forth For God" Tune: GENEVA 124

---

1. For a closing response following the benediction during June and July, sing verse one of "[Blessed][Blest] Be The Tie That Binds" (Tune: DENNIS).

Proper 7
Sunday between June 19 and June 25 inclusive

First Lesson: Genesis 21:8-21
Theme: Even If ... God Is Present

Call To Worship

Leader: God is present, lift up your hearts.
People: God is with us.
Leader: God is present, let your soul be still.
People: God is with us.
Leader: Come worship and be glad for God is good.
All: Alleluia, God is with us indeed.

Collect

You have taught us, O God with ample mercy, about the breadth of your compassion. Keep us always aware that there is a greater perspective and understanding than our own. Guide us toward serenity of faith in you, O God. Amen.

Prayer Of Confession

All: Sometimes, like Sarah, we succumb to jealousy and demand the extreme.
Leader: Still, you listen, O God.
All: Sometimes, like Abraham, we become caught in the dilemma.
Leader: Still, you lead us, O God.
All: Sometimes, like Hagar when most desperate, we give in to hopelessness.
Leader: Still, you provide, O God.
All: Praise be to God. Amen.

42A Hymns[1]

"Be [Calm][Still], My Soul" Tune: FINLANDIA
"Lift Up Your [Heads][Hearts]" Tune: WOODLANDS
"Lead Us, Heavenly Father, Lead Us" Tune: DULCE CARMEN

Proper 7
Sunday between June 19 and June 25 inclusive

Second Lesson: Romans 6:1b-11
Theme: In Newness Of Life

Call To Worship
Come and worship God. Hear again the good news about baptism, the outward sign of God's gift of grace. Walk in the newness of life that happens because of baptism. Know again the hope of our oneness as the body of Christ.

Collect
Gracious God, each time we witness a baptism, we remember about our own participation in this sacrament. In your Spirit, we move beyond death. Our lives change. We find life. We know the comfort of union with you, O God. In the name of Christ. Amen.

Prayer Of Confession
We ask senseless questions sometimes, God. If your grace is so free, then why do we have to worry about sin? We can repeatedly do the wrong, then come to church and ask forgiveness. Remind us, God, that when we sin, we separate ourselves from the best within us, from healthy relationships with others, and from oneness with you. When we are alive to you in Jesus Christ through baptism, every dimension of our life reflects newness of life. Amen.

42A Hymns[1]
"Not Alone For Mighty Empire" Tune: AUSTRIAN HYMN
"We Would See Jesus, Lo His Star Is Shining" Tune: CUSHMAN
"Make Me A Captive, Lord" Tune: LLANLLYFNI

Proper 7
Sunday between June 19 and June 25 inclusive

Gospel: Matthew 10:24-39
Theme: Net Gain

Call To Worship
"Those who find their life will lose it, and those who lose their life for my sake will find it." These difficult words of Jesus invite us to take another look at what we lose and what we find as we live in Jesus' way.

Collect
We praise you, O God, for offering us the hope of new beginnings. What we gain in spirit far overpowers the weight we lose. Thanks be to God. Amen.

Prayer Of Confession
We want you to consider us worthy, O God, but the idea of letting go of and losing our lives for your sake overwhelms us. It must have overwhelmed those of Jesus' day who sometimes had to surrender their physical lives. We would rather someone else would do it. Lead us, O God, toward a fuller understanding of the transformation of the spirit. In the name of Christ. Amen.

42A Hymns[1]
"This Is A Day Of New Beginnings" Tune: BEGINNINGS
"God's Eye Is On The Sparrow" Tune: SPARROW
"Awake, My Soul And With The Sun" Tune: MORNING HYMN

---

1. For the summer months, consider a weekly "congregational choice" hymn.

Proper 8
Sunday between June 26 and July 2 inclusive

First Lesson: Genesis 22:1-14
Theme: The Right Call

Call To Worship

Leader: Why have you come to church today?
People: We are here because we have heard the right call.
Leader: Come, listen, and observe. Be attentive to the word of God.
People: Praise be to God.

Collect

If we are going to believe, O God, then we need to act on that belief. We are here to connect faith and belief with responsibility. We are here to look again at our gifts and talents and to offer them to you in service, for we are yours, O God. Amen.

Prayer Of Confession

Dare we say to you, O God of great plans, "Here I am"? These words might get us into great trouble. These words might turn our lives completely around. These words might mark the adventure of a new beginning. If we choose to dare, help us to be ready. In the name of Christ. Amen.

43A Hymns

"Here I Am, Lord" Tune: HERE I AM, LORD **OR** "I Am [Thine][Yours], O Lord" Tune: I AM YOURS
"Take My Gifts" Tune: TALAVERA TERRACE or HOLY MANNA **OR** "Take My Life [God,][And] Let It Be" Tune: VIENNA
"Christian, Rise And Act [Thy][Your] Creed" Tune: INNOCENTS

Proper 8
Sunday between June 26 and July 2 inclusive

Second Lesson: Romans 6:12-23
Theme: Your Wages?

Call To Worship

The free gift of life means that in our low moments we no longer need to dwell on fear. God's grace brings peace to our hearts so we can live fully now. Do these words sound like a dream, too good to be true? They are words from God. Praise be to God.

Collect

We present ourselves to you, O God, as those you have brought from death to life. From the depths of our hearts, we become increasingly obedient to the forms of teaching to which you entrust us. In the name of Christ. Amen.

Prayer Of Confession

We know, Gracious God, that the force of sin still exists in the world. We rejoice that, as the result of your grace, sin need not have the upper hand. Help us to make the right choices and to live in ways that reflect allegiance to your goodness, O God. Amen.

43A Hymns

"Glorious Things Of [Thee][You] Are Spoken" Tune: AUSTRIAN HYMN
"How Deep The Silence Of The Soul" Tune: TALLIS' THIRD TUNE
"Let Justice Flow Like Streams" Tune: ST. THOMAS

Proper 8
Sunday between June 26 and July 2 inclusive

Gospel: Matthew 10:40-42
Theme: In Jesus' Name

Call To Worship

Leader: How do you greet? Do you see everyone as worthy of Christian love?

People: The supermarket clerk, the shopkeeper, the bank teller?

Leader: The phone solicitor, the parking attendant, the rent collector?

People: A parent, a daughter, a son, a lifemate?

Leader: Let us greet one another as through the eyes of Jesus Christ.

Collect

We come to this place of holy welcoming to receive your welcome, O God, in the name of Christ. In turn, we welcome your presence in our lives. May our welcoming become contagious with approval, acceptance, and appreciation. In Jesus' name. Amen.

Prayer Of Confession

When we forget to look with the eyes of a Christian, O God, we turn into judgers and prejudgers. We miss the rewards of joy. Let us become seekers of small ways to welcome others with love. In Jesus' name. Amen.

43A Hymns

"Jesus, Friend, So Kind And Gentle" Tune: SICILIAN MARINERS
"My Song Is Love Unknown" Tune: RHOSYMEDRE
"Jesus, Thou Divine Companion" Tune: PLEADING SAVIOR

Proper 9
Sunday between July 3 and July 9 inclusive

First Lesson: Genesis 24:34-38, 42-49, 58-67
Theme: Lifemate

Call To Worship
Not only did Isaac take Rebekah as his wife according to custom, but he also chose to love her. In a different time, in our land of freedom, we choose our partners in other ways. However, the truths of mutual respect and responsibility still hold today within this freedom.

Collect
"Will you go with this person?" "I will." We delight in the willingness of voluntary responsibility, O God. We applaud those who dare in our difficult social times to give a covenantal relationship a try. We rejoice when two persons so venture and are willing to work out a partnership of ever-deepening commitment. Amen.

Prayer Of Confession
Are you a matchmaker for us, God? Do you bring us together with our lifemates? When we feel external pressures or sense an interior urgency to grow a lasting relationship, give us the patience to wait, even if it takes longer than we want. We ask for wisdom to listen to and with our whole being. Be with us as part of the voice of inner wisdom we can trust, O God. In Jesus' name. Amen.

44A Hymns[1]
"God Send Us Men Whose Aim 'Twill Be" Tune: MELROSE **OR**
"Judge Eternal, Throned In Splendor" Tune: RHUDDLAN
"Go, My Children, With My Blessing" Tune: AR HYD Y NOS **OR**
"When Love Is Found" Tune: O WALY WALY
"O God, Beneath Thy Guiding Hand" Tune: DUKE STREET

135

Proper 9
Sunday between July 3 and July 9 inclusive

Second Lesson: Romans 7:15-25a
Theme: Freedom or License?

Call To Worship
As we enter into an attitude of worship today, let us be mindful of the laws which belong to God, the laws that are made by society, and the rules we ourselves invent when we stretch the gift of freedom too far.

Collect
Gracious God, grant us the honesty to discern which among the rules we live by are ours and which are God's. Grant us the humility to see beyond self-interest. Guide us as we practice the tenacity of stretching past ourselves. In the name of Jesus the Christ. Amen.

Prayer Of Confession
While we pray together, the prayer of confession is still a personal prayer. Let us, then, confess to God: I do not always understand my own actions. For I do not do what I want and know is right, but I do the very thing I hate. I can will what is right, but I cannot always do it. Forgive me for taking such license with the freedom you have given me, O God. Help me to do better. Amen.

44A Hymns[1]
"Dear [God, Embracing][Lord And Father] Of [Humankind] [Mankind]" Tune: REST
"What A Friend We Have In Jesus" Tune: ERIE [CONVERSE]
"We Shall Overcome" Tune: WE SHALL OVERCOME

Proper 9
Sunday between July 3 and July 9 inclusive

Gospel: Matthew 11:16-19, 25-30
Theme: Come To Me

Call To Worship
"Come to me, all you that are weary and are carrying heavy burdens," Jesus said, "and I will give you rest. Take my yoke upon you, and learn from me; for I am gentle and humble in heart, and you will find rest for your souls. For my yoke is easy, and my burden is light."

Collect
No matter who we are, dear God, Jesus' invitation to come to him with the weary, burdened part of ourselves brings comfort and rest for our souls. All can come. We are grateful. Amen.

Prayer Of Confession
Leader: Gracious, Compassionate God, we bring you our weariness and our heavy burdens —
People: Help carry the weight, O God, of those trying to manage chronic health problems.
Leader: Help us carry the heaviness of meeting workloads and time limits without sufficient respite.
People: Help us carry the weight, O God, of raising a family and of being youths in these times.
Leader: Help us bear the burden of grief.
All: We would have your comfort and rest for our souls. Amen.

44A Hymns
"[O Come To Me, You Weary][The Voice Of God Is Calling]" Tune: MEIRIONYDD **OR** "We Yearn, O [Christ][Lord], For Wholeness" Tune: PASSION CHORALE
"Stand By Me" Tune: STAND BY ME
"Sing Them Over Again To Me" Tune: WORDS OF LIFE

---

1. On the remaining Sundays of summer, use the first verse of "Take My Life And Let It Be Consecrated" (Tune: VIENNA) as a closing response.

Proper 10
Sunday between July 10 and July 16 inclusive

First Lesson: Genesis 25:19-34
Theme: Isaac and Rebekah

Call To Worship
If Isaac was forty years old when he and Rebekah married and the twins were not born until Isaac was sixty, the couple must have had tremendous staying power. As we worship today, let us remember all among us — relatives, friends, and others — who have struggled with or are presently trying to grow babies.

Collect
We embrace in prayer, O God, all who ache with unfulfilled hopes. Let our prayers speak daily to you about them. Through Jesus. Amen.

Prayer Of Confession
Our prayers go to those who want children but find having them difficult. When the twins struggled within Rebekah's womb, Rebekah's depression was even more intense than during the previous two decades. "If it is to be this way, why do I live?" she asked God. To survive, she must have felt accepted and cherished by Isaac. Like Rebekah and Isaac, dear God, we want so much and we try so hard; then when it might become possible, we are scared to death that something will go wrong. We wonder if, after all, it were a mistake. Be especially present to the Rebekahs and Isaacs of today. Amen

45A Hymns
"God Of Grace And God Of Glory" Tune: CWM RHONDDA
"If [Thou][You] But Suffer God To Guide [Thee][You]" Tune: NEUMARK [WER NUR DEN LIEBEN GOTT]
"Have Faith In God, My Heart" Tune: SOUTHWELL

Proper 10
Sunday between July 10 and July 16 inclusive

Second Lesson: Romans 8:1-11
Theme: Root Of Life

Call To Worship
Set your mind on the Spirit. Then you will find life and peace. If Christ is in you, it makes no difference that the bodily part of you will die. Do not worry about these things. God will give you life through God's Spirit living within you.

Collect
As we learn to live and walk according to the Spirit, O God, our confidence grows that you are with us in all of life and in life after death. We rejoice in this freedom of hope through Jesus the Christ. Amen.

Prayer Of Confession
We often choose, O God, to set our minds on things of the flesh. Then we end up focusing on the wrong things. We sputter about what we do not possess. We fret about possible outcomes of health problems rather than treasuring what we can do today. Encourage us to set our minds on the things of the Spirit, O God. Guide us so we might live and walk according to your Spirit. Amen.

45A Hymns
"O Praise The Gracious Power" Tune: CHRISTPRAISE RAY
"O Holy Spirit, Root Of Life" Tune: PUER NOBIS NASCITUR
"We Want To Learn To Live In Love" Tune: CANONBURY

Proper 10
Sunday between July 10 and July 16 inclusive

Gospel: Matthew 13:1-9, 18-23
Theme: Humus

Call To Worship
Wind blows away seed sown on a path. Seed has no chance to penetrate rocky ground with roots. Weeds overtake seed sown among thorns. However, humus offers seed the necessary components for germination, sustenance, and the bearing of fruit. Let us be like fertile compost so we might be well-prepared to hear, receive, and bring to fruition God's will for us on earth.

Collect
God who hears us, we would turn our ear to you. God who listens to what we have to say, we would listen with our whole selves. God who nourishes and sustains us, we would care for the truths you offer as tenderly as for a newly planted seedling. For the sake of Jesus the Christ. Amen.

Prayer Of Confession
Gracious God, we rush into the lure of quick joy only to find that it fuels a superficial life. Guide us toward the establishment of solid roots so that our faith will not run out of steam. Lead us, Holy One, away from the shallow and toward the enduring qualities. In Jesus' name. Amen.

45A Hymns
"Lead On [Eternal Sovereign][O King Eternal]" Tune: LANCASHIRE
"God Be In My Head" Tune: LYTLINGTON
"Once To Every Man And Nation" Tune: EBENEZER

Proper 11
Sunday between July 17 and July 23 inclusive

First Lesson: Genesis 28:10-19a
Theme: Know This

Call To Worship

Leader: God says to us, "Know that I am with you and will keep you wherever you go" —

People: In a move to a new town, when beginning a new position, starting high school, the first kindergarten day, daring to do something for the first time.

Leader: God says to us, "Know that I am with you and will keep you wherever you go" —

People: In routine's humdrum, during tough decision-making, in the aftermath of divorce, in the middle of grief, throughout radiation and chemotherapy, at each monitoring of blood glucose, amid utter frustration.

All: In all of life, God says to us, "Know that I am with you and will keep you wherever you go."

Collect

Open our eyes, Sustaining God, that we may see evidence of your presence in all our living. Amen.

Prayer Of Confession

We forget, O God, that, as with Jacob, you will not leave us until you have done as you promised. We wish your instructions for us were as clear as those you spoke to the leaders in the Old Testament. Help us trust your presence as we grapple with hard decisions and confront difficult life situations. Help us trust that your wisdom will show itself through our own integrity. In Jesus' Name. Amen.

46A Hymns

"How Firm A Foundation" Tune: FOUNDATION or ADESTE FIDELES

"God's Eye Is On The Sparrow" Tune: SPARROW **OR** "Open My Eyes" Tune: OPEN MY EYES

"Holy God, We Praise [Thy][Your] Name" Tune: GROSSER GOTT, WIR LOBEN DICH

141

Proper 11
Sunday between July 17 and July 23 inclusive

Second Lesson: Romans 8:12-25
Theme: Adopted Hope

Call To Worship
If we hope for what we do not see, we wait with patience. So be of good courage. Take in stride present suffering. Do not think you must know everything right now. Why, you ask. All who are led by the Spirit of God are God's adopted children. Come, let us be people of hope. Let us rejoice as the family of the living God.

Collect
We relax within, O God, because we know that we who live by the Spirit are yours. We live toward the future with an attitude of hope. Praise be to you, O God, our Creator and our Sustainer. Amen.

Prayer Of Confession
Holy Parent, open our hearts to feel love and acceptance through your Spirit. Give strength to our hope when courage wilts. Infuse joy into our energy, the joy that we are yours, you whom we call Father/Mother because of Jesus Christ. Amen.

46A Hymns
"Joyful, Joyful We Adore [Thee][You]" Tune: HYMN TO JOY
"Spirit Of God Descend Upon My Heart" Tune: MORECAMBE
"Every Time I Feel The Spirit" Tune: AFRICAN AMERICAN SPIRITUAL

Proper 11
Sunday between July 17 and July 23 inclusive

Gospel: Matthew 13:24-30, 36-43
Theme: The Right Time

Call To Worship
In a Chicago community garden that looked like a weed patch, wise youths had interplanted a weed to screen a lucrative crop of garden greens. At the right time, they harvested the weeds and took the sheltered crop to market. Let us consider today the right time for nurture and the right time for harvest.

Collect
We come here, O Wise One, knowing that you readily discern what is weed and what is wheat. We accept that we have little control over the negative dimensions that slip into our lives. Thank you for teaching us that even in the midst of trouble, in your realm the good can prevail. For Christ's sake. Amen.

Prayer Of Confession
More important, O God, than immediately culling the troublesome elements is protecting the treasure from accidental harm. Help us to tend the positive, fruitful parts of ourselves, our church, and our community so that we will be ready at harvest time. In the name of Jesus. Amen.

46A Hymns
"[Sois la Semilla][You Are The Seed]" Tune: ID Y ENSEÑAD
"New Every Morning Is The Love" Tune: MELCOMBE
"Christ Will Come Again" Tune: IDA

Proper 12
Sunday between July 24 and July 30 inclusive

First Lesson: Genesis 29:15-28
Theme: Apprentice

Call To Worship
Leader: Remember that God still guides us today. God always finds
            new ways of shedding light on our paths. We rejoice in an
            ever-present, ever-creating, and ever-sustaining God.
People: Praise be to God.

Collect
God of purpose, God of design, God who knows the way: We
come with open hearts ready to hear your word. We come as students
of faith. We come as your disciples. Through Christ. Amen.

Prayer Of Confession
What unexpected apprenticeships we find ourselves serving, dear
God. As you enabled Jacob to be constant, strengthen us as you work
out your purpose for us. Despite unsavory or disreputable designs of
others, help us to proceed with your plans in a single-minded posture.
In the name of Christ. Amen.

47A Hymns
"God Of The Earth, The Sky, The Sea" Tune: HERR JESU CHRIST
OR "God Who Madest Earth And Heaven" AR HYD Y NOS
"[All][He] Who Would Valiant Be" Tune: ST. DUNSTAN'S **OR**
"Remember God Was Guiding" Tune: WEBB
"God Is Working His Purpose Out" Tune: PURPOSE

Proper 12
Sunday between July 24 and July 30 inclusive

Second Lesson: Romans 8:26-39
Theme: Convinced

Call To Worship

Leader: For I am convinced that neither death, nor life, nor angels, nor rulers,

People: Nor things present, nor things to come, nor powers, nor height, nor depth,

Leader: Nor anything else in all creation will be able to separate us from the love of God in Christ Jesus our Lord.

People: We are convinced. Praise be to our merciful and compassionate God.

Collect

Thou, who answers our sighs with your own,

Thou, who searches our hearts and knows what is on our minds,

Thou, who is for us and assures us that all things work together for good,

Thou.

Prayer Of Confession

So convincing is your compassion, that our questions melt. So close you are, O God, that we need not speak. So comforting is your presence, that our hearts grow still and know that you are God. Amen.

47A Hymns

"We Bear The Strain Of Earthly Care" Tune: HERMON **OR** "We Are Often Tossed And Driven" or "We'll Understand It Better By And By" Tune: BY AND BY

"Prayer Is The Soul's Sincere Desire" Tune: ST. AGNES

"By Gracious Powers" Tune: BONHOEFFER INTERCESSOR

Proper 12
Sunday between July 24 and July 30 inclusive

Gospel: Matthew 13:31-33, 44-52
Theme: Most Important

Call To Worship

Leader: Good things may come in small packets:
People: Seeds, seeds, and more seeds.
Leader: A little stretches and stretches:
People: Seeds, seeds, and more seeds.
Leader: What surprise and mystery one seed holds as we await its germination:
All: The kingdom of God is like the tiny mustard seed that someone took and sowed in a field.

Collect

How mysteriously you work, O God, to show us that as precious as is the smallest seed, it is nothing unless we take it in hand and plant it. We promise to pay attention to the tiniest seeds of hope in our relationships. We vow to do our part in giving them a chance to sprout. We will keep ourselves open to greet the surprises of the realm of God. In the name of Christ. Amen.

Prayer Of Confession

God of the mustard seed and a few grains of yeast, we succumb to thinking greedily about quantity when even the smallest bit used in faith yields a fine result. Remind us to live wholeheartedly by treasuring what we have. Remind us to use what is available with faith and a clear mission so we might experience better your realm. Through Jesus the Christ. Amen.

47A Hymns

"God Moves In A Mysterious Way" Tune: DUNDEE
"[God][Lord], Speak To Me, That I May Speak" Tune: CANONBURY
"We Would Be Building" Tune: FINLANDIA

Proper 13
Sunday between July 31 and August 6 inclusive

First Lesson: Genesis 32:22-31
Theme: Bless Me?

Call To Worship
Leader: "Bless me?" you ask.
People: Bless us, we say, because we need the assurance that someone is for us.
Leader: "Bless me?"
People: Bless us, we say, for we need to know you notice we are doing the best we can.
Leader: "Bless me?"
People: Bless us, we say, so we might have enough courage to continue the journey.

Collect
Giver of blessing, we acknowledge your importance in our lives. We do not and cannot make it through this life depending entirely upon our own stamina. We are grateful, God, those times we become aware of your presence and your blessing. In the name of Christ. Amen.

Prayer Of Confession
Dare we ask for your blessing, God, when we seem left alone in the midst of the struggle? When we win? When we feel that life is defeating us? What qualifies us for your blessing? Surely not our limited perspective. Is your blessing something to earn? Is it an act of your faith in us? Dare we, like Jacob, ask for your blessing, or must we wait until you volunteer it for your own reasons? Amen.

48A Hymns
"Fight The Good Fight" Tune: PENTECOST
"We Are Climbing Jacob's Ladder" or a duet of "We Are Climbing Jacob's Ladder" (men) alternating with "We Are Dancing Sarah's Circle" (women) Tune: JACOB'S LADDER
"Lord, Dismiss Us With Your Blessing" Tune: SICILIAN MARINERS **OR** "Go, My Children, With My Blessing" Tune: AR HYD Y NOS

Proper 13
Sunday between July 31 and August 6 inclusive

Second Lesson: Romans 9:1-5
Theme: Discouraged

Call To Worship

Plans do not always go as we would have them. Come, all who are discouraged. Come, all who feel that you have failed. Come, all who are hopeless. Come to this place where you will be loved and accepted as you are. Come to this place of transformation.

Collect

Our prayers go to you, O Listening, Compassionate Parent. We pray for all whom hindrances impede. We pray for all who lack the energy of spirit to persevere. Be with us, sustain us, and lead us back to paths of health. We ask in Jesus' name. Amen.

Prayer Of Confession

When we despair from the difficulties of our entrusted tasks, guide our thoughts toward your blessing, O God. When discouragement overwhelms us, show us again the signs of your promises and the evidence of your having adopted us as your own. Through Jesus the Christ. Amen.

48A Hymns

"Lift Up Your Heads, [O][Ye] Mighty Gates" Tune: TRURO
"Count Your Blessings" Tune: BLESSINGS
"Love Lifted Me" Tune: SAFETY **OR** "There Is A Balm In Gilead" Tune: BALM IN GILEAD

Proper 13
Sunday between July 31 and August 6 inclusive

Gospel: Matthew 14:13-21
Theme: Just A Minute

Call To Worship
Learning of the beheading of his friend John the Baptist, Jesus wanted to withdraw and mourn alone. Instead, he fed the multitudes. By this he taught us that compassionate concern for others is stronger than the magnet of needing time for ourselves. We are here today for ourselves so that we might find Christ-like vitality to provide compassionate care when others need us.

Collect
We are here, O God, ready for you to fill us with your love. Even as we pause, we prepare to serve others. We are grateful for this time to refresh the spirit. In the name of Christ. Amen.

Prayer Of Confession
We ask for just a minute to stop and catch the breath. We who carry the responsibilities of being blessed as Christians hear the call to live beyond ourselves. Nourish our spirits, Gracious God, so we might feed those with impoverished spirits. Let us share together the holy meal given by Christ for all. Amen.

48A Hymns
"Blessed Are The Poor In Spirit" Tune: ANNIKA'S DANCE **OR**
   "Break [Now][Thou] the Bread of Life" Tune: BREAD OF LIFE
"We Are Not Our Own" Tune: YARNTON
"Jesu, Jesu, Fill Us With Your Love" Tune: CHEREPONI

Proper 14
Sunday between August 7 and August 13 inclusive

First Lesson: Genesis 37:1-4, 12-28
Theme: Peace At Home First

Call To Worship

Leader: Look to your families, what do you see?
People: We see both dissension and cooperation.
Leader: Look to your families, what do you see?
People: We see both jealousy and adoration.
Leader: Look, what do you see?
People: We see ourselves both falling short and making valid efforts to do our best.
Leader: Come now with all the complexities of human relationships to this place of grace.

Collect

Let our dedication to peace be stronger than our need to fight, dear God. Let our sense of fairness be greater than our craving to be first. Let our appreciation of justice transcend our sense of jealous competition. O God, our guide and our savior. Amen.

Prayer Of Confession

We know, Gracious God, that peace begins at home. When discord bellows in the house or conflict disquiets our souls, all we do elsewhere reflects its chaos. Strengthen our courage, God, to come to terms with the turmoil in our own lives so we might better bring peace wherever we go. Amen.

49A Hymns

"God Of Grace And God Of Glory" Tune: CWM RHONDDA
"I Need Thee Every Hour" Tune: NEED
"Let There Be Peace On Earth" Tune: WORLD PEACE

Proper 14
Sunday between August 7 and August 13 inclusive

Second Lesson: Romans 10:5-15
Theme: With Heart And Voice

Call To Worship

Leader: Believe with your heart and confess with your voice.
People: Jesus is Christ. God is in charge.
Leader: Believe with your heart and confess with your voice.
People: All who call on God's name shall be saved.
All: Believe with your heart and confess with your voice. Let us praise God.

Collect

There is a song in the air, O Holy Savior. It sings a tune for you. The tune is of faith. The tune is of love. How beautiful is our song of good news. Hear the song of our hearts, O God. Amen.

Prayer Of Confession

We do not want someone else telling us how to believe, O God, so we hesitate to speak of our faith to others. Help us remember that we need not set bonfires when it only takes a spark to spread your love. Let the expressions on our faces, the way we are with people, and the way we behave give voice to what we believe in our hearts. In the name of Christ. Amen.

49A Hymns

"God Is Here" Tune: ABBOT'S LEIGH
"Immortal Love, Forever Full" Tune: BEATITUDO or SERENITY
"It Only Takes A Spark" Tune: PASS IT ON

151

Proper 14
Sunday between August 7 and August 13 inclusive

Gospel: Matthew 14:22-33
Theme: Turbulence

Call To Worship
Like the turbulence of storm waves tossing a small boat, the commotion of unexpected happenings causes an uproar of squalls in our lives. We are here to remember God's present guidance throughout the furor.

Collect
We come as Peter with deliberate faith. We come as Peter with a surprising absence of faith. Despite the human, mercurial nature of our faith, Gracious God, we also confess, "Jesus, truly you are the Son of God." Amen.

Prayer Of Confession
So often, dear God, we have faith in theory but not in reality. Help us to move beyond hypothesis and toward the practice of faith. We ask through Jesus whose extended hand invites us to move forward with him. Amen.

49A Hymns
"Guide My Feet" Tune: GUIDE MY FEET
"Who Trusts In God, A Strong Abode" Tune: BISHOPGARTH or WAS MEIN GOTT WILL
"Within The Maddening Maze Of Things" Tune: SONG 67

Proper 15
Sunday between August 14 and August 20 inclusive

First Lesson: Genesis 45:1-15
Theme: The Sound Of Mercy

Call To Worship

Leader: To reconcile is to preserve life.
People: We would be forgiving.
Leader: To bring unity is to lay aside noisy replay of past actions.
People: We would be forgiving.
Leader: To compose our differences is to choose to forgive.
People: We would forgive.
All: Let us worship God.

Collect

The sound of mercy is a silence pregnant with the possibility of our moving forward again. The sound of mercy is a song continually resolving discord. We see you at work, Merciful Creator, in the life of Joseph once sold by his brothers. We see you at work in each act of forgiveness that we initiate. Praise be to you, O God. Amen.

Prayer Of Confession

God of mercy, we acknowledge that it is easier to prolong discord than to settle things. The game of lording it over others appears fun at first. The pseudo-power of keeping things negatively stirred up falsely exalts us. Forgive us, God. Help us to overcome the urge to rule others. Teach us the art of self-forgiveness that frees us from the circling distress of self-hate and moves us toward the freedom to be kind. In the name of Jesus the Christ. Amen.

50A Hymns

"For The Beauty Of The Earth" Tune: DIX
"Father, Almighty, Bless Us" Tune: INTEGER VITAE
"All Praise [Be Yours][To Thee], My God This Night" Tune: TALLIS'
    CANON

Proper 15
Sunday between August 14 and August 20 inclusive

Second Lesson: Romans 11:1-2a, 29-32
Theme: Assurance

Call To Worship
What must be mysterious to children is how parents can discipline them without jeopardizing their love for them. As a parent disciplines a contrary child, so God holds us responsible for our actions. Discipline is part of God's love. Rejection or discard as garbage is not. Be reassured and give thanks to our loving God.

Collect
Irrevocable, unchangeable, irreversible, and final. These are the words of your love for us, O God. These are the words of your gifts to us. Love is how you call us your own. Love speaks of your mercy because of our disobedience. What a divine mystery is your love, O God. In the name of Christ. Amen.

Prayer Of Confession
We push your patience, Holy Parent, as we elbow our limits. Forgive us. Enable us to sense your mercy so that we will try to clean up our lives. For the sake of Christ. Amen.

50A Hymns
"Blessed Assurance" Tune: ASSURANCE
"I Know Not How That Bethlehem's Babe" Tune: BANGOR
"And Have You Never Known?" Tune: DIADEMATA or ICH HALTE TREULICH STILL

Proper 15
Sunday between August 14 and August 20 inclusive

Gospel: Matthew 15:(10-20) 21-28
Theme: Conduit For God

Call To Worship
What words come out of your mouth? What do your thousand tongues sing? Are your words an invitation to a relationship of kindness? How does what you say echo what is in your heart?

Collect
We would speak words that nourish and encourage, O God. We would speak words that build up and support. Wherever we go, we would be conduits for justice and for your peace. In the name of Christ. Amen.

Prayer Of Confession
When we pay attention to the wrong things, O God, for the wrong reasons, help us to take greater care. Let our words include rather than exclude others. Let our embrace adopt what is fair rather than reject what is different. In Jesus' name. Amen.

50A Hymns
"[O][Oh] For A Thousand Tongues To Sing" Tune: AZMON
"[God][Lord], Speak To Me That I May Speak" Tune: CANONBURY
    OR "Into My Heart, Lord Jesus" Response
"Alleluia! Alleluia! Hearts To Heaven" Tune: HYFRYDOL or
    WEISSE FLAGGEN

Proper 16
Sunday between August 21 and August 27 inclusive

First Lesson: Exodus 1:8—2:10
Theme: Unique Talents

Call To Worship

Today we celebrate the lives of two Hebrew midwives, Shiphrah and Puah. We lift up with joy the mother of Moses and his sister, Miriam. Come, let us cheer the cleverness of all who survive under the weight of injustice and persecution.

Collect

For the shrewdness of mind you have given the oppressed Israelites of long ago and those not so long ago, O God, we praise you. For the capacity of Israelite women to meet cunning with equal ingenuity while surviving injustice, we praise you. For the ability to use our talents to overcome adversity, we praise your holy name. Amen.

Prayer Of Confession

Leader: In homes of spousal abuse,
People: Wherever others enslave others, hear our prayer for justice and for the survival of the human spirit.
Leader: Behind doors of rooms of seniors,
People: Wherever others enslave others, hear our prayer for justice and for the survival of the human spirit.
Leader: In places where youngsters are treated as things,
People: Wherever others enslave others, hear our ...
Leader: Where medical insurance is not a reality,
People: Wherever others enslave others, hear our ...
Leader: Where working people of any age are kept in poverty because of the greed of others,
All: Wherever others enslave others, hear our prayer for justice and for the survival of the human spirit. Amen.

51A Hymns

"In Egypt Under Pharaoh" Tune: LANCASHIRE
"Lord Of Our Life, And God Of Our Salvation" Tune: CLOISTERS or ISTE CONFESSOR (ROUEN)
"The Voice Of God Is Calling" Tune: MEIRIONYDD

Proper 16
Sunday between August 21 and August 27 inclusive

Second Lesson: Romans 12:1-8
Theme: Diversity

Call To Worship
Let us worship God by honoring the diversity of talents among us. Let us worship God by using our abilities in ways that are holy and acceptable to God. Let us worship God in the offering of ourselves to fulfill God's will for us in this world. Amen.

Collect
In your design of creation, O God, you have filled the human pallet with boundless varieties of ability. Grant us increasing acumen to identify and admit to our talents. Grant us the energy of challenge to use these gifts wisely and in ways acceptable to you. Amen.

Prayer Of Confession
We suppose, dear God, that we will last forever. We take for granted that valued talents will extend lifelong. Lessen our disappointment when life accidents change our bodies and other circumstances abort the use of cherished abilities. Help us to avoid squandering our gifts while we own them. Help us to discern and cultivate previously unrecognized talents as our situations change. Amen.

51A Hymns
"Breathe On Me, Breath Of God" Tune: TRENTHAM
"We Are The Church" Tune: PORT JERVIS
"Forward Through The Ages" Tune: ST. GERTRUDE

Proper 16
Sunday between August 21 and August 27 inclusive

Gospel: Matthew 16:13-20
Theme: Dare To Proclaim

Call To Worship

Come worship and be joyful. We recognize that Jesus is the Son of the living God. Christ is risen. The Holy Spirit is with us today and every day, here and everywhere. Come worship, people of God, and be joyful.

Collect

For the gift of inner hearing and seeing that Jesus is the Messiah and that we are the church, we give you thanks, O God. Amen.

Prayer Of Confession

Like Peter, we confess that we believe in Jesus. We whisper our confession lest others think we are silly or outmoded or showing off. We speak our confession to our inner selves and profess our belief with the mechanical, unison voice of a worship time affirmation. Let us look Jesus in the eye, as Peter must have, and declare beyond secret with his firm and steady voice, "You, Jesus, are the Messiah, the Son of the living God." Hear our words, O God. Amen.

51A Hymns

"O God, We Praise Thee, And Confess" Tune: TALLIS' ORDINAL
"[Incarnate God][Strong Son Of God], Immortal Love" Tune: ROCKINGHAM
"Hail To The Lord's Anointed" Tune: ROCKPORT

Proper 17
Sunday between August 28 and September 3 inclusive

First Lesson: Exodus 3:1-15
Theme: Holy Ground, Therefore ...

Call To Worship[1]

Leader: The place on which you are standing is holy ground, therefore,

People: Love one another with mutual affection; outdo one another in showing honor.

Leader: Holy ground. Therefore,

People: Rejoice in hope, be patient in suffering, persevere in prayer.

Leader: Holy ground. Therefore,

People: Live in harmony with one another.

Leader: Holy ground. Therefore,

People: Do not be overcome by evil, but overcome evil with good.

Leader: The place on which you are standing is holy ground, therefore,

All: If it is possible, so far as it depends on you, live peaceably with all.

Collect

Help us, O God, to recognize holy ground in all of our living. Amen.

Prayer Of Confession

Forgive us, O God, for profaning the holy ground of human relationships when we fail to listen with our hearts to others. Forgive us for desecrating the holy ground of mother earth when we do not take care of our natural resources. Forgive us, God, for dishonoring the holy ground of ourselves when we neglect our mental, physical, and emotional health. Amen.

52A Hymns

"Where Cross The Crowded Ways Of Life" Tune: GERMANY
"Won't You Let Me Be Your Servant?" Tune: SERVANT SONG **OR**
    "Help Us Accept Each Other" Tune: ACCEPTANCE or AURELIA
"[How][O] Beautiful, [Our][For] Spacious Skies" MATERNA

---

1. From The First And Second Lessons: Exodus 3:1-15; Romans 12:9-21.

159

Proper 17
Sunday between August 28 and September 3 inclusive

Second Lesson: Romans 12:9-21
Theme: Thirty-One Policies

Call To Worship
Do you think being a Christian is like joining an organization?
Are you ready for the strategy for being Christian? Come, let us start
over again and again at the lifelong project of being Christian.

Collect
We praise you, O God, for creating people like Paul of Tarsus who
understood that being a Christian exacts a total life change. We hope,
O God, to honor this way of life as encompassing all aspects of our
relationships with you, with our neighbor, and with ourselves. In the
name of Christ. Amen.

Prayer Of Confession
Thirty-one guidelines from Paul to follow if we choose to be Christian, dear God. That is too much to ask. As with all impossible tasks,
help us to make being Christian manageable by concentrating first on
one or two guidelines. Help us accept our fallings short by remembering your free "try again" of grace. Amen.

52A Hymns
"All My Hope On God Is Founded" Tune: MEINE HOFFNUNG
"Lord, Thy Mercy Now Entreating" Tune: RINGE RECHT
"Your Ways Are Not Our Own" Tune: SCHUMANN

Proper 17
Sunday between August 28 and September 3 inclusive

Gospel: Matthew 16:21-28
Theme: Disciples

Call To Worship

Leader: Jesus said, "If any want to become my followers, let them deny themselves and take up their cross and follow me."

People: We have come here to follow Jesus.

Leader: Jesus said, "For those who want to save their life will lose it, and those who lose their life for my sake will find it."

People: We have come here to be disciples of Christ.

Collect

We have only commenced to understand the cost of discipleship, O God. We have only begun to grasp its joy. Praise be to you, O God of life. Amen.

Prayer Of Confession

We begin to sense, O God, that when we stand on holy ground, everything changes. Like Peter who knew he would lose Jesus, the higher the price, the more we also resist. Help us to avoid getting in our own way. For the sake of Jesus. Amen.

52A Hymns

"O Be Joyful In The Lord" Tune: ROCK OF AGES
"Lord, We Thank Thee For Our Brothers" Tune: AUSTRIAN HYMN
"Jesus Calls Us O'er The Tumult" Tune: GALILEE or ST. ANDREW

Proper 18
Sunday between September 4 and September 10 inclusive

First Lesson: Exodus 12:1-14
Theme: Together

Call To Worship
Like Hebrews of Aaron's and Moses' time, called at the first Passover to gather as families and share the sacrificed lamb of a goat or sheep, this congregation also is called to worship together as a family. Come, let us worship our sustaining God with praise and thanksgiving.

Collect
We lift our prayers today for those in other places who must make secret marks to identify their faith. We pray that they might have a robust sense of community and the spiritual sustenance of a shared symbolic meal. Amen.

Prayer Of Confession
How do we make a sign, dear God, that tells you we belong to you? Is the sign a shouting billboard? Is it a whispered moment of the soul? You would note both, for we are yours. Yet, even we, like the early Hebrews, must take the initiative of first confessing that we are part of the community of faith. In Christ's name. Amen.

53A Hymns[1]
"Before Jehovah's [Aweful][Awesome] Throne" Tune: PARK STREET or WINCHESTER NEW
"O Thou Great Friend" Tune: FFIGYSBREN
"Rise Up, O [Church][Men] Of God" Tune: FESTAL SONG

Proper 18
Sunday between September 4 and September 10 inclusive

Second Lesson: Romans 13:8-14
Theme: How To Live

Call To Worship

Leader: Love does no wrong to a neighbor.
People: Love is thoughtful to classmates.
Leader: Love does no wrong to a neighbor.
**People: Love waits patiently in a conversation with a neighbor
of a different first language.**
Leader: Love does no wrong to a neighbor.
People: Love pays attention to what happens in the neighborhood.
Leader: Love does no wrong to a neighbor.
People: Love practices fair play in the workplace.

Collect

On this day of considering the workers of our land, we pray, O
God, for all who serve as mediators, that they might see each worker
as their neighbor. Give to those who attempt to reconcile worker with
worker the perception to recognize Christ in each one. Impart to all
workers a sense of enthusiasm for what they do and a sense of dignity
because of their efforts. Give to supervisors the ability to encourage
and convey appreciation for work well done. Amen.

Prayer Of Confession

We live in times, dear God, when it is safer and less complicated to
avoid our neighbors. Somehow, not caring for a neighbor makes us
lesser people. Enable us to recognize who is a neighbor. Help us to
take small, tender steps toward being neighborly as we meet people
face to face. Let a neighborly attitude light up our eyes and counte-
nance our expressions at home, at school, in the workplace, and in the
shop. We pray in the name of Jesus the Christ. Amen.

53A Hymns[1]

"Come, Labor On" Tune: ORA LABORA
"God's Action, Always Good And Just" Tune: WAS GOTT TUT **OR**
    "God's Glory Is A Wondrous Thing" Tune: HUMMEL
"God Be With You" Tune: GOD BE WITH YOU

Proper 18
Sunday between September 4 and September 10 inclusive

Gospel: Matthew 18:15-20
Theme: Two Or Three

Call To Worship

Leader: With two or three gathered in Christ's name,
People: We enter this place of worship to meet God.
Leader: With two or three gathered in Christ's name,
People: We expand our capacity to love.
Leader: Where two or three are gathered,
People: We witness truth together.
All: **Where two or three are gathered in Christ's name, God is here among us.**

Collect

We learn here, O God, the holy spirit of community. Be among us. Clarify our sense of purpose and our understanding of the faith. In the name of Jesus the Christ. Amen.

Prayer Of Confession

We can accomplish many but not all things alone, Gracious God. We stand still in our efforts when we cannot resolve all struggles single-handedly. Prompt us, O God, to remember the strength of your Holy Spirit when two or three gather in your name. Amen.

53A Hymns[1]

"When Morning Gilds The Skies" Tune: LAUDES DOMINI
"Draw Us In The Spirit's Tether" Tune: UNION SEMINARY **OR**
    "We Gather Together" Tune: KREMSER
"Through The Night Of Doubt And Sorrow" Tune: ST. ASAPH

---

1. In the next four weeks, sing verse four of "Amazing Grace" (Tune: AMAZING GRACE) (My God has promised good to me/whose words my hope secures/God will my shield and portion be/as long as life endures) as a closing response after the benediction. See NCH.

164

Proper 19
Sunday between September 11 and September 17 inclusive

First Lesson: Exodus 14:19-31
Theme: Trust

Call To Worship
Leader: We come to worship because we want to trust in God.
People: Unless we trust in God, our faith is hollow.
Leader: God waits for us here and invites our trust.
People: Let us trust in God and renew our courage.

Collect
Like a pillar of cloud, O God, you stand between us and trouble. Your presence is so real it lights up the darkness. Like dividing water, you cut a path through the sea of our chaos. If we but trust in you, you guide us. Amen.

Prayer Of Confession
You have shown yourself again and again as one who keeps promises. You said you would guide the Israelites and you did. Forgive us when we do not think to put our trust in you. When trusting is hardest, show us that it is more important than anything else we do. Give us the courage to let you be our guide. Amen.

54A Hymns
"If [You][Thou] But Trust In God To Guide [Thee][You]" Tune: NEUMARK [WER NUR DEN LIEBEN GOTT]
"Lord Of All Being, Throned Afar" Tune: LOUVAN
"God Of Our Life, Through All The Circling Years" Tune: SANDON

165

Proper 19
Sunday between September 11 and September 17 inclusive

Second Lesson: Romans 14:1-12
Theme: Opinions

Call To Worship
Let us sing of the mighty power of God. Let us praise the maker of all creation. Come, let us worship God.

Collect
We worship you, God, knowing that you, not we, are the center. We pledge to turn our focus toward you in all matters. We promise to remember you are with us and will try to do better in talking things over with you. Amen.

Prayer Of Confession
Merciful God, we fail to consider others' opinions. Forgive our insensitivity. We tend to think we are always right, even while knowing in our hearts that we are not. Forgive our arrogance. We pass judgment on our brothers and sisters. Forgive our meddling. Guide us, O God, in living beyond ourselves. Help us to remember that to you, alone, we are accountable. Amen.

54A Hymns
"[I][We] Sing The [Almighty][Mighty] Power Of God" Tune: ELLACOMBE or FOREST GREEN
"Shadow And Substance" Tune: TWILIGHT **OR** "Have Thine Own Way, Lord" Tune: ADELAIDE
"Praise To The Living God" or "Maker, In Whom We Live" Tune: DIADEMATA

Proper 19
Sunday between September 11 and September 17 inclusive

Gospel: Matthew 18:21-35
Theme: Forgiven

Call To Worship

Leader: How long must we wait, God,
People: For people to stop fighting —
Leader: Nations with nations,
People: Buyers and sellers,
Leader: The big ones and the little ones,
People: In-laws and relatives,
Leader: Husbands and wives,
People: Sisters and brothers,
All: For me to stop fighting with me?

Collect

We pray for nations to forgive nations, to lift the science of government to the art of recognizing and appreciating a people. We pray for nations to practice persistent compassion beyond sporadic, self-serving whims of mercy. We pray for nations to understand nations, to be big-hearted for the right reasons. Amen.

Prayer Of Confession

Again and again, we can confess to you, O Merciful God, knowing that we will be forgiven. Your forgiving us is pointless if we do not practice forgiving others in turn. Encourage our growth toward being forgiving persons. In Jesus' name. Amen.

54A Hymns

"Father Eternal, Ruler Of Creation"[1] Tune: LANGHAM
"Spirit Of Jesus, If I Love My Neighbor" Tune: BENJAMIN
"Praise The Lord! Ye Heavens, Adore Him" Tune: HYFRYDOL

---

1. Consider singing a successive verse of "Father Eternal, Ruler Of Creation" each Sunday until World Communion Sunday when all verses might be sung as a communion hymn.

Proper 20
Sunday between September 18 and September 24 inclusive

First Lesson: Exodus 16:2-15
Theme: Provide

Call To Worship
We come to this place carrying many anxieties, worries, and griev-ances. Know that God hears our complaints. Rest in the certainty that God provides. Let us worship God.

Collect
We praise you, Holy Parent, for your ability to move us beyond disquiet and complaint. We praise you for providing what we need each day. Amen.

Prayer Of Confession
We always want more, O God. Something greedy within us hun-gers far beyond what we require. Teach us to live like Type 2 diabet-ics who, as they learn to eat within the processing capability of a faulty pancreas, discover smaller amounts of food sustain and satisfy. Quiet our craving to live a week or year ahead. Teach us to direct our atten-tion to today. Help us turn around the despair of uncertainty and trea-sure each morsel of food as a gift of sustenance and hope. Amen.

55A Hymns[1]
"He Leadeth Me" Tune: HE LEADETH ME
"Great Is [Thy][Your] Faithfulness" Tune: FAITHFULNESS
"[Be Not Dismayed][God Will Take Care Of You]" Tune: MARTIN

Proper 20
Sunday between September 18 and September 24 inclusive

Second Lesson: Philippians 1:21-30
Theme: Live

Call To Worship

Leader: Softly and tenderly you beckon, Jesus.
People: We speak for those who wrestle with diseases that will consume their lives.
Leader: Softly and tenderly you beckon, Jesus.
People: We speak for those who struggle with intimidating chronic conditions.
Leader: Softly and tenderly you beckon, Jesus.
People: We speak for those who want prematurely to escape, who mistakenly think their life is over.
Leader: Softly and tenderly you beckon, Jesus.
People: We speak for those who have given up and for those who refuse to give in.
All: We speak for all who are caught between the will to die and the will to live.

Collect

When we ask should I or should I not, turn our thoughts, O God, to how we can best serve you. How can we be of greatest help to those we would leave behind? When we ask how much longer, God, turn our question to what we run from that makes your call inviting. When we meet those for whom the push toward death draws stronger than the pull toward life, let our responses be understanding rather than condemnation, acceptance rather than judgment, and compassion rather than reproach. In the spirit of Christ. Amen.

Prayer Of Confession

Help us, Compassionate God, to distinguish between needing a breather and needing to leave life behind. Help us separate boredom from exhaustion, lethargy from struggle-spent, and indifference from life-tired. Give us the courage to let go when the struggle is over. Refresh us when renewal is possible. In the name of Christ. Amen.

55A Hymns[1]

"Jesus, I Live To You" Tune: LAKE ENON

"Softly And Tenderly" Tune: SOFTLY AND TENDERLY [THOMP-SON] **OR** "Precious Lord, Take My Hand" Tune: PRECIOUS LORD

"Holy Spirit, Truth Divine" Tune: MERCY or VIENNA

Proper 20
Sunday between September 18 and September 24 inclusive

Gospel: Matthew 20:1-16
Theme: Work

Call To Worship

Leader: Why do you work?
People: To pay the bills and put food on the table. To do our part in sharing responsibilities.
Leader: Why do you work?
People: To have something meaningful and fulfilling to do. To benefit others because of our efforts.
Leader: Why do you work?
People: To learn and hone the skills of our talents. To honor the gifts God has given us.

Collect

We come to you, O God, as those whose work is fulfilling vocation and as those for whom the thought of work brings frustration. We stand before you as those unable to work and as those sized down beneath their stature. Together we come, Benevolent Sustainer, some grumbling and grouching and others swelling sighs of gratitude. Thank you for understanding us. In the name of Jesus the Christ. Amen.

Prayer Of Confession

We think, O Generous One, that we need much more than we actually do. Many whose incomes exceed what we require feel empty because we have forgotten to share. Many whose incomes fall short somehow make do. Some among us are impoverished of things but plentiful of spirit. Help us all to keep money in proper perspective. Help us manage the funds we have and keep in focus our intent to live and work as meaningfully as we are able. Amen.

55A Hymns[1]

"In Christ There Is No East Or West" Tune: ST. PETER or McKEE
"[Born][Son] Of God, Eternal Savior" Tune: WEISSE FLAGGEN
"Dear [Master][Jesus], In Whose Life I See" Tune: O JESU CHRISTE,
    WAHRES LICHT or HURSLEY

---

1. Consider singing the response "Lead Me, Lord" as a preface to the pastoral prayer each worship day through Proper 25.

Proper 21
Sunday between September 25 and October 1 inclusive

First Lesson: Exodus 17:1-7
Theme: Are You Here, God?

Call To Worship
Take time out to be with God. Come to this place where God will defend you. Come here to restore your soul. Come to heal and to gain strength so you might leave able to defend and restore others.

Collect
You are here, God, when we need you as well as when we are oblivious to our needs. You stand ready to fortify us with the miracles of your common sense and your vantage point. We meet this day with the certainty and comfort of receiving your presence. Through Jesus the Christ. Amen.

Prayer Of Confession
We approach the day with high hopes, then find reality tempers the ideal. When complaints repeatedly trounce on us, we get to wandering around in personal wildernesses, God. We need defending. We need someone with us who will not make things worse. As you answered Moses, we also need you, O God, to respond to our cries of "What shall I do?" Be for us, be near, we pray. Amen.

56A Hymns
"God Of [Our Fathers][The Ages Past]" Tune: NATIONAL HYMN
"Lord, Save The World" or "Creator Of The Earth And Skies" Tune: UFFINGHAM
"May The Sending One Defend You" Tune: ROLLINGBAY

Proper 21
Sunday between September 25 and October 1 inclusive

Second Lesson: Philippians 2:1-13
Theme: Commitment

Call To Worship
Hear the challenge to take an active part in our relationship to God: Holy Scripture says to work out your own salvation with fear and trembling, for it is God who is at work in you, enabling you both to will and to work for God's good pleasure.

Collect
We come humbly and fully human before you, O God. We come obedient before you, O God, ready to assist you here on earth. We come receptive before you, O God, open to respond to the distresses of others. For the sake of Christ. Amen.

Prayer Of Confession
We ask, gracious God, to find enough encouragement in Christ to make Christ our center rather than ourselves. Show us that it is you who is at work in us, urging us to please you by our convictions and through our actions. In Jesus' name. Amen.

56A Hymns
"Take My Life, [God,][And] Let It Be" Tune: MESSIAH or VIENNA
"O How I Love Jesus" or "There Is A Name I Love To Hear" Tune: O HOW I LOVE JESUS
"Heart And Mind, Possessions, Lord" Tune: TANA MANA DHANA
   OR "The Gift Of Love" Tune: GIFT OF LOVE

Proper 21
Sunday between September 25 and October 1 inclusive

Gospel: Matthew 21:23-32
Theme: Authority

Call To Worship

Why do you come to church? Seemingly obedient to God's authority, some of us come to worship regularly but are inattentive. Others worship infrequently but want the church to be there for us when we need it. Some show up when we are needed for a task. Who is your highest authority? Do you respect God's authority in this year of your life? What does the authority of God mean to you?

Collect

Gracious God, creator of all life and author of our lives, to you we give highest power. May your spirit of holiness encircle us as we honor you. In the spirit of Christ. Amen.

Prayer Of Confession

There is hope for us sinners. The hope lies in our willingness to think again, to reconsider, and to turn around our ways and change. Is there hope also for those who give lip service to the faith? Help us all to sing your name, O God, by our actions as well as our mouths. Amen.

56A Hymns

"Praise To The Lord, The Almighty" Tune: LOBE DEN HERREN
"I To The Hills Will Lift [Mine][My] Eyes" Tune: DUNDEE
"Come, [Now][Thou] Almighty King" Tune: ITALIAN HYMN

Proper 22
Sunday between October 2 and October 8 inclusive

First Lesson: Exodus 20:1-4, 7-9, 12-20
Theme: Ten Commandments

Call To Worship
Leader: The truths of God endure.
People: Come, let us worship God.

Collect
All praise to you, O God, for caring enough about your ongoing creation to offer us direction for our living. Help us honor you by following the commandments that teach us how to live in relation to you. Help us honor those around us by observing your rules for living among others. Amen.

Prayer Of Confession
Because we are human, Holy Parent, we fall short of our intentions. Lead us toward developing a strong sense of what is right and within conscience. Strengthen us so that when we fail we will have the boldness to try again to follow higher principles. As taught to us by Jesus Christ. Amen.

57A Hymns[1]
"Praise To The Living God" Tune: DIADEMATA **OR** "[O][Oh] Worship The King][We Worship You, God]" Tune: LYONS
"O My Soul, Bless [Your Creator][God, The Father]" Tune: STUTTGART
"We Limit Not The Truth Of God" or "Thou God Of All, Whose Spirit Moves" Tune: OLD 22ND

Proper 22
Sunday between October 2 and October 8 inclusive

Second Lesson: Philippians 3:4b-14
Theme: Credentials

Call To Worship
Leader: What qualifies you to be called a Christian?
People: Jesus loves me, this I know.
Leader: What are your credentials? Wherein lies your confidence?
People: Jesus loves me, this I know.
All: Jesus loves us, this we know.

Collect
You, O God, have made us your own through the life, death, and resurrection of Jesus Christ. You have made us your own because of your love. Your love is the source of our confidence and faith. Praise be to you, O God. Amen.

Prayer Of Confession
As we make knowing Christ our goal, guide our thoughts away from our own lists of qualifications, O God, and toward Christ. Let us put into proper perspective personal assets and gains lest they hinder the goal of becoming Christ-like. Help us to live toward this future. Amen.

57A Hymns[1]
"More Love To [Thee][You]" Tune: MORE LOVE TO THEE
"My Song Is Love Unknown" Tune: RHOSYMEDRE
"Jesus Loves Me" Tune: JESUS LOVES ME

Proper 22
Sunday between October 2 and October 8 inclusive

Gospel: Matthew 21:33-46
Theme: God's Authority

Call To Worship
God's realm is filled with surprise. We cannot always comprehend what God has in mind because we are not God. Come here to worship knowing that the Creator continually works out the design of caring and creation.

Collect
When your actions seem unfair and baffling to us, O God, guide us toward asking how we are not producing the fruits of your realm. Guide us toward yielding a proper harvest. For Christ's sake. Amen.

Prayer Of Confession
We go about doing as we have always done, O God. We act with good conscience. We take for granted doing things according to our plans and forget that you may have something entirely different in mind for us. Help us to remember that you author the realm of God. Amen.

57A Hymns[1]
"Christ Is Made The Sure Foundation" Tune: REGENT SQUARE
"For The Healing Of The Nations" Tune: CWM RHONDDA
"Christian, Rise And Act [Thy][Your] Creed" Tune: INNOCENTS

---

1. As a closing response after the benediction in October, sing verse one of "Give Up Your Anxious Pains" (Tune: ICH HALTE TREULICH STILL).

Proper 23
Sunday between October 9 and October 15 inclusive

First Lesson: Exodus 32:1-14
Theme: I Love You

Call To Worship
Can you imagine God having a divine temper tantrum? When Aaron's play at leadership resulted in the molten calf, God's wrath came close to exploding. But Moses implored and Moses prompted and God changed his mind.

Collect
Here, O God, we can remind one another of the promises we have made on the chancel steps — promises at baptism or christening, at confirmation, of marriage or partnership, of church membership, of commission to carry out an important task. No matter how bad things become, we can come here, renew our promises, and begin again. Amen.

Prayer Of Confession
Leader: Why don't you just give up on us, God?

Middle Of Life Persons: We are so wrapped up in our own lives. It's do this and do that and money, money, and more money, God. It's things and more things. Whenever we do get a moment, all we can think about is play.

People: Why don't you just give up on us, God?

Leader: I love you, says God.

Youths: We force our limits most of the time. We defy, we rebel, we resist, God.

People: Why don't you just give up on us, God?

Leader: I love you, says God.

Oldest Persons: We want to be finished with responsibility. We won't live forever, God. We're held together by metal and tenacity.

People: Why don't you just give up on us, God?

Leader: I love you, says God.

All: God loves. Amen.

178

58A Hymns

"All Praise To Our Redeeming Lord" Tune: ARMENIA

"Depth Of Mercy" Tune: CANTERBURY **OR** "Father In Heaven, Who Lovest All" Tune: SAXBY

"O Spirit Of The Living God" Tune: FOREST GREEN or MELCOMBE

Proper 23
Sunday between October 9 and October 15 inclusive

Second Lesson: Philippians 4:1-9
Theme: Rejoice

Call To Worship
One way to stand firm in our faith is to focus on the strengths of positive attitude. Look for what is worthy of praise. Lay aside worry. Respond with gentleness. Concentrate on what is true, honorable, just, pure, pleasing, and commendable. These are the words of the writer of the letter to the church at Philippi. What if we were to carry this counsel into our homes, schools, businesses, and places of work today?

Collect
In times of increasing criticism and ballooning of petty concerns, Christians have the advantage of a hopeful perspective. We gather at this place of worship determined to keep on doing the things that we learn here about you, dear God, so that your peace, which surpasses all understanding, might guard our hearts and our minds in Christ Jesus. Amen.

Prayer Of Confession
The wisdom of our faith offers practical guidance for living beyond the doors of this sanctuary. We are grateful for your counsel, O God. We pray that we might hold on to these truths so they will have a chance to influence our lives and the lives of those around us. Amen.

58A Hymns
"The God Of Abraham Praise" Tune: LEONI
"Grant Us Wisdom To Perceive You" Tune: QUEM PASTORES **OR**
    "To Love Just Those Who Love You" Tune: PASSION CHORALE
"Whate'er [My][Our] God Ordains Is Right" Tune: WAS GOTT TUT

Proper 23
Sunday between October 9 and October 15 inclusive

Gospel: Matthew 22:1-14
Theme: Disciple?

Call To Worship

Leader: The call is to worship God.

People: Sometimes we fail to take God seriously.

Leader: The call is to become worthy before God.

People: Sometimes we do not care and miss out.

Leader: What we expect may be far different from God's idea of discipleship.

People: Sometimes we do not listen.

All: We would listen with our hearts and hear.

Collect

We see, O God, that in being chosen, we also make a choice. We see that to become a disciple requires discipleship. We see that to become worthy before you, O God, we, as you do, must set aside our unworthiness. For the sake of Christ. Amen.

Prayer Of Confession

All: How do we know when you have called us, God? We might read the signs as wishful thinking. Someone else's invitation? What if we follow but are not prepared? How do we know when you have chosen us, O God? So many questions come with discipleship. How do we know what you have in mind? How could we possibly be worthy?

Leader: Know that God's realm is filled with surprises.

58A Hymns

"Rejoice, O People, In The Mounting Years" Tune: YORKSHIRE
"As We Gather At Your Table" Tune: BEACH SPRING
"Take Time To Be Holy" Tune: HOLINESS or SLANE

181

Proper 24
Sunday between October 16 and October 22 inclusive

First Lesson: Exodus 33:12-23
Theme: Invisible

Call To Worship

Leader: God's presence goes with us
People: Into the territories of leadership — the boardroom, the conference, the classroom.
Leader: God's presence goes with us
People: Into areas of trailblazing — parenting, growing a marriage, building a new career.
Leader: Through all our journeys, God's presence goes with us.
All: Praise be to God.

Collect

Gracious God who knows us tenderly by name, to you we turn with praise and adoration. Although we cannot perceive you through earthly senses, we want to accept the possibility of your existence. Although we muse at times that you are the invention of our needs, we choose to believe that you are greater than us alone. We are not the deities, you are the one true God. Amen.

Prayer Of Confession

When we cannot see into others' eyes, at first we distrust them. We wonder what they conceal from us. We do not want you to be invisible, O God. We want to see your face. We think we need to look into your eyes in order to know you, soul to soul. Teach us that other trust with heart contact coming beyond sensory perception. Teach us to listen. Teach us to look around us for evidence of your presence. Give us the courage to accept knowing you only in part. Amen.

59A Hymns

"[O][Our] God, To Whom We Turn" Tune: STEADFAST **OR** "Creating God, Your Fingers Trace" Tune: KEDRON

"God [Himself Is][Is Truly] With Us" or "God Himself Is Present" Tune: ARNSBERG (WUNDERBARER KONIG) **OR** "God, Whose Love Is Reigning O'er Us" Tune: LAUDA ANIMA

"Softly And Tenderly" Tune: SOFTLY AND TENDERLY [THOMPSON]

Proper 24
Sunday between October 16 and October 22 inclusive

Second Lesson: 1 Thessalonians 1:1-10
Theme: One By One

Call To Worship
Grace to you, people of this congregation. We give thanks to God for all of you and mention you in our prayers. We remember your works of faith, your labors of love, and the steadfastness of your hope. Peace to you, people of God.

Collect
Through the word, you come to us one by one, Holy Sustainer. You reveal your nearness through the unique empowerment of each of us. You show your presence through the Holy Spirit. One by one, we offer this gathering of thanks and gratitude. In the name of Jesus, our Savior. Amen.

Prayer Of Confession
When we hear again, dear God, that others call us by name in prayers to you, we feel that we do count. When we see that others have noticed the most modest of our loving labors, we know a sustenance that renews the soul's energy. We as a congregation are the church, O God, yet this church can be nothing without individual members. We would ask to be gentle locators of hope, tender uncoverers of hidden faith, and encouragers among those who are trying to transform their hope and their faith into actions that reflect service to you, O God. Amen.

59A Hymns
"Praise, O Praise Our God And King" Tune: MONKLAND
"O Brother Man, Fold To Thy Heart Thy Brother" or "Children Of God" Tune: INTERCESSOR or WELWYN
"Awake, My Soul, Stretch Every Nerve" Tune: CHRISTMAS

Proper 24
Sunday between October 16 and October 22 inclusive

Gospel: Matthew 22:15-22
Theme: Visible

Call To Worship

Leader: We assemble as people of a faith.

People: We live as citizens of a community.

Leader: We belong to the family of God which encompasses all time and space.

People: We belong to a neighborhood that stretches across a world of time zones.

All: We are connected to this world but also anticipate another realm.

Collect

We find signs of your presence, O God, wherever people are, for your realm knows no unholy place. It is we, not you, who divide the world into categories of the secular and the holy. It is we, not you, who play political games with each other. We pray that we might decrease our hypocritical habits as we increase our dedication to be true in all areas of living to what we profess in church. In the name of Christ. Amen.

Prayer Of Confession

God, grant us the wisdom to know when to separate from the things that are God's what belongs to the secular world. Let us keep our values in proper place so we avoid worshiping society as a lesser God. Give us the courage to avoid succumbing to distracting traps that others set for us. Give us the wisdom to recognize, then to dismiss, their negative games. Help us speak for what we know to be right rather than compromise our beliefs. We ask in Jesus' name. Amen.

59A Hymns

"Here, O My Lord, I See [Thee][You] Face To Face" Tune: LANGRAN
"Jesus, Where'er Thy People Meet" Tune: FEDERAL STREET
"I Love [Thy][Your] Kingdom, Lord" Tune: ST. THOMAS

Proper 25
Sunday between October 23 and October 29 inclusive

First Lesson: Deuteronomy 34:1-12
Theme: Growing Up

Call To Worship

Leader: Like Joshua of old, we are full of the spirit of wisdom because of those who have gone before us.

People: We enter the millennium with delicately patterned heirlooms of attitude.

Leader: We come with a heritage of experience.

People: We bring the collected learning of science and medicine, of experiment and proof.

Leader: We come with the certainty of being the people of God.

All: We approach the future as the people of God.

Collect

Gracious God, we are grateful for a generous heritage of mentors. Guide us so that we in turn might provide a quality of leadership that will encourage a world of higher morals and values. In the spirit of Christ. Amen.

Prayer Of Confession

Assuming leadership calls for springing beyond hurdles of dependency, diffident reluctance to dare, and sluggish following of others. As we lead, O God, we trust your infusion into our hearts of a proper measure of perspective so we might balance tradition with vision. Amen.

60A Hymns

"God, We Thank You For Our People" or "God Who Stretched The Spangled Heavens" Tune: HOLY MANNA

"Take My Gifts" or "Take My Life, And Let It Be Consecrated" Tune: HOLY MANNA, TALAVERA TERRACE, or VIENNA

"God, Whose Giving Knows No Ending" or "Glorious Things Of [Thee][You] Are Spoken" Tune: AUSTRIAN HYMN

Proper 25
Sunday between October 23 and October 29 inclusive

Second Lesson: 1 Thessalonians 2:1-8
Theme: Sharing Ourselves

Call To Worship

Leader: Let us care for each other as Jesus would. Let us seek the brokenhearted and others needing a gentle word. Let us dare to share ourselves as well as the message of the church.

People: Let us worship our God and our Sustainer.

Collect

Despite weaknesses and shortcomings, O God, we live our faith in community. Despite set goals and careful designs, plans stray. We look to you, therefore, for strength to maintain a balance of the actual with the ambition. Amen.

Prayer Of Confession

Gracious God, let the courage fueling our leadership ventures spring from right motives. Help us to set aside opposition as well as greed, flattery, and praise-seeking. Remind us that we chose to follow Christ and we were chosen to be Christians today for a reason. In our efforts to manage the church, help us guard against becoming so organized that we hold people at a distance, so involved in telling the messages of our faith that we forget to live them. In the spirit of Jesus Christ. Amen.

60A Hymns

"Jesus, With Thy Church Abide" Tune: VIENNA
"Make Me A Captive, Lord" Tune: LLANLLYFNI
"In The Cross Of Christ I Glory" Tune: RATHBUN

Proper 25
Sunday between October 23 and October 29 inclusive

Gospel: Matthew 22:34-46
Theme: Love

Call To Worship
As we gather for worship today, hear again the words of Jesus Christ: Love the Lord your God with all your heart, and with all your soul, and with all your mind. Love your neighbor as yourself. All else in our faith hangs on these two commandments.

Collect
Holy Parent of Jesus the Christ and our Parent, we desire to deepen our comprehension of what it means to love you. Because we are from you, we want to become more adept at loving ourselves. Let growth of empathy go hand in hand with loving our neighbor. Amen.

Prayer Of Confession
God, teach me to ask first if a particular action reflects my loving you with my whole being — with heart, soul, and mind. Teach me next to ask, does this action reveal both that I love myself and that I act out of love toward my neighbor? I am determined to focus my life upon these two great commandments with your help and in the name of Jesus. Amen.

60A Hymns
"Glory Be To God On High" Tune: GWALCHMAI
"[All][He] Who Would Valiant Be" Tune: ST. DUNSTAN'S
"Jesus, Thou Divine Companion" Tune: PLEADING SAVIOR

Proper 26
Sunday between October 30 and November 5 inclusive

First Lesson: Joshua 3:7-17
Theme: Miracles of Leadership

Call To Worship

In the miracle of leadership, we do not lead alone. We choose our committees, delegates, and representatives. We are aware of a silent partnership with God. Come, let us worship in the strength of this living God.

Collect

As we consider the miracles of leadership, we strive to balance responsible actions with your grace, O God. We marvel at human community that thrives with artful leadership. We are grateful for your presence among us. Amen.

Prayer Of Confession

We are grateful that you provide by pushing back many waves for us, O God. Grant us continued strength to stand by our decisions. Help us distinguish guidance from direction and suggestion from command. Help us listen with open ears of faith. In the name of Jesus. Amen.

61A Hymns

"Forth In [Thy][Your] Name, O Lord, I Go" Tune: MORNING HYMN
   or DUKE STREET
"O Lord And Master Of Us All" Tune: ST. AGNES or WALSALL
"O Word Of God Incarnate" Tune: MUNICH

Proper 26
Sunday between October 30 and November 5 inclusive

Second Lesson: 1 Thessalonians 2:9-13
Theme: The Holy Guest

Call To Worship
Let us remember God's word at work in each of us. Let us notice and accept God's company. In all we do, let us give evidence of our faith in this holy guest. Come, let us worship God.

Collect
We praise you, O God, for your faithfulness to your people. We are grateful for your being in charge still in these times. We proclaim your wonderful name. Through Jesus the Christ. Amen.

Prayer Of Confession
We are aware that you, O God, know all that we think and do. We can be better witnesses. We could be leading a more worthy life. Forgive us when we do not care. Forgive us when we lose sight of what is right. Thank you for continuing to thrust us toward a higher level of living. In the name of Christ. Amen.

61A Hymns
"Let Us [All] With [A] Gladsome Mind" Tune: INNOCENTS
"[Ye][You] Servants Of God" Tune: HANOVER
"Forth In [Thy][Your] Name, O Lord, I Go" Tune: MORNING HYMN
    or DUKE STREET

Proper 26
Sunday between October 30 and November 5 inclusive

Gospel: Matthew 23:1-12
Theme: A Humble Style

Call To Worship
We gather today to ponder how to serve God and humankind as leaders. We would bring our attitudes of service as close as possible to that of the servant, Jesus of Nazareth. Come, let us worship God.

Collect
In Jesus, you have given us a model of leadership to follow, O God. Be our vision, be our wisdom, as we set goals of service and bring them to fruition. Through Christ. Amen.

Prayer Of Confession
We want to have enough pride, God, to call it a healthy self-esteem. Yet we hope to avoid haughtiness or arrogance. Help us ignore position and title as we serve you and those around us. We want to carry enough humility to remember who we are. Yet we must escape traps of self-abasement or useless submissiveness. Guide us in keeping these qualities of character in proper balance as we serve you by leading. Amen.

61A Hymns
"Christ, Whose Glory Fills The Skies" Tune: RATISBON
"Love Divine, All Loves Excelling" Tune: BEECHER or HYFRYDOL
"Be [Now][Thou] My Vision" Tune: SLANE

190

Proper 27
Sunday between November 6 and November 12 inclusive

First Lesson: Joshua 24:1-3a, 14-25
Theme: As For Me And My Household

Call To Worship

Leader: Choose this day whom you will serve, God or some lesser god.

People: We will serve God. We come to serve God with sincerity and faithfulness.

Collect

O God, we come as households and families of many definitions to reaffirm our commitment to you. Like Joshua of old, we, too, promise, "As for me and my household, we will serve God." Amen.

Prayer Of Confession

The god of money, the god of prestige, the god of snobbery, of advanced degrees, of arrogance, football, self — these lesser gods we also know, O Holy One. Help us keep them in their place. Give us the tenacity to honor you. Through Christ. Amen.

62A Hymns

"[O][Oh] For A Thousand Tongues To Sing" Tune: AZMON

"O For A Closer Bond With God" Tune: BEATITUDO **OR** "O For A Heart To Praise My God" Tune: RICHMOND

"Guide My Feet" Tune: GUIDE MY FEET **OR** "O Jesus, I Have Promised" Tune: ANGEL'S STORY

Proper 27
Sunday between November 6 and November 12 inclusive

Second Lesson: 1 Thessalonians 4:13-18
Theme: Hope's Gift

Call To Worship
In this time between autumnal splashes of color and Advent's resurrection of hope, skeletal trees and faded grass gloom our thoughts toward death. Come to worship today appreciating God's gift to the faithful of an immutable comfort.

Collect
God of grace, we praise you for your gift of hope. We are grateful that Jesus' death was for all people of the household in all time — those who knew nothing about him, his contemporaries, and all who have come and will come after his day. Our encouragement enters as sighs of relief because you save us all from our sinful selves. All glory be to you, O God. Amen.

Prayer Of Confession
In bleak moments of unbelief, dear God, we ponder what will happen to us after we die. Some who have known suffering wonder if we will ever know peace or wholeness. Some who knowingly have gone against what is right envision the possible consequences after death. Help us remember, Holy Parent, that you alone are present with us in all things, through all matters, and beyond all time. Despite what we have done, and how we have been, you remain with us all, O Thou Triune God. Amen.

62A Hymns
"Immortal, Invisible, God Only Wise" Tune: ST. DENIO
"Still, Still With Thee" Tune: CONSOLATION
"Eternal Father, Strong To Save" Tune: MELITA

192

Proper 27
Sunday between November 6 and November 12 inclusive

Gospel: Matthew 25:1-13
Theme: Be Prepared

Call To Worship

Leader: Come, pay attention.
People: Listen up.
Leader: Come, make ready.
People: Anticipate, now.
Leader: Come, prepare.
People: Be wise.

Collect

God, our prayer is to grow in our sense of responsibility in all realms of life — health, work, and church. We would focus on what is important. We would do the necessary things ahead of time to be ready. We would be wise. In the Spirit of Christ. Amen.

Prayer Of Confession

Gracious God, we put off things until the last moment. Sometimes we squeeze by. Other times, we are too late and lose. We act without thinking, then wonder why things go wrong. We are passive when the call is to act. Help us greet with strong habits of preparation the anticipated changes in our lives so that encounters with the unexpected might be more facile. Amen.

62A Hymns

"I Greet Thee, Who My Sure Redeemer Art" Tune: SONG 24
"Lead, Kindly Light, Amid The Circling Gloom" or "Unto The Hills We Lift Our Longing Eyes" Tune: LUX BENIGNA or SANDON
"With Songs And Honors Sounding Loud" Tune: ELLACOMBE

Proper 28
Sunday between November 13 and November 19 inclusive

First Lesson: Judges 4:1-7
Theme: Judge

Call To Worship
Like Deborah, the Israelite judge, we are called upon to reflect, to discuss, and to make decisions that lead to action. We have heard that we should not judge lest we be judged. However, there is a time for judgment when we are asked and after we have deliberated. Come, let us worship God.

Collect
So that we might move closer to becoming at one with you, O Just God, without spilling a drop of blood, guide our deliberations and our decision making, that we might increase fairness and justness in an unfair and unjust world. In the name of Christ. Amen.

Prayer Of Confession
Grateful for the respect of being asked to offer an opinion, we ask what Christ would have done. As we influence others with increasing accountability and responsibility, we seek patient wisdom to listen. We would hear all sides of an issue, think about it, and debate it before jumping to a decision. Be with us, O God. Amen.

63A Hymns
"Who Trusts In God A Strong Abode" Tune: BISHOPGARTH or WAS MEIN GOTT WILL
"Teach Me, My God And King" Tune: MORNINGTON
"These Things Shall Be" Tune: TRURO

Proper 28
Sunday between November 13 and November 19 inclusive

Second Lesson: 1 Thessalonians 5:1-11
Theme: Clothed For Salvation

Call To Worship
Leader: We can only encourage one another and build up each other when we ourselves know courage and worth, therefore,
People: Be children of light and children of the day.
Leader: Therefore,
People: Stay awake and be sober.
Leader: Therefore,
People: Put on the breastplate of faith and love.
Leader: Therefore,
People: For a helmet, put on the hope of salvation.

Collect
Our aim, O God, is for alertness which comes from being strong of body, spirit, and mind rather than defensive, self-protective tension that stands ready to spring or flee. We, therefore, appreciate the sustenance of this community of faith and love and the hope of salvation through Christ. Amen.

Prayer Of Confession
Gracious God, we hope to become less vulnerable to the unexpected by living within a community of courage and support. Help us to do our part in this community of faith by concentrating on chosen treasures of faith, love, and the hope of salvation. Give us the strength to stay as healthy as possible in mind, body, and soul. For your sake. Amen.

63A Hymns
"O God Of Earth And Altar" Tune: LLANGLOFFAN
"Father, In Thy Mysterious Presence" Tune: DONNE SECOURS
"O Day Of God, Draw Near" Tune: ST. MICHAEL

Proper 28
Sunday between November 13 and November 19 inclusive

Gospel: Matthew 25:14-30
Theme: In A Few Things

Call To Worship
We think that the small, seemingly insignificant things we do remain unnoticed. Then the story about the talents reaches us. Every effort counts. We come here today to rededicate our striving to be trustworthy stewards of each of God's gifts.

Collect
We want to be known, O God, as people who try. We want to be known as people who avoid wasting our abilities. Let industry, not fear, govern our actions. In Christ's name, we pray. Amen.

Prayer Of Confession
If we can be trusted in a few things according to our abilities, then we will be trustworthy in many things. Start small, prove yourself, do the apprenticeship and the internship, get your foot in the door — these lesser things count for much in God's eye. Bolster our stamina, Holy Parent, for doing the small things. Transform our understanding of preparation as also training in integrity. Amen.

63A Hymns
"[Mine][My] Eyes Have Seen The Glory" Tune: BATTLE HYMN OF THE REPUBLIC

"O [Master][Savior], Let Me Walk With [Thee][You]" Tune: MARYTON

"O How Glorious, Full Of Wonder" Tune: IN BABILONE or HYMN TO JOY

Proper 29 (Christ The King)
Sunday between November 20 and November 26 inclusive

First Lesson: Ezekiel 34:11-16, 20-24
Theme: Shepherd

Call To Worship

Leader: God said: As shepherds seek out their flocks when they are among their scattered sheep, so I will seek out my sheep.

People: Will you find us, God, when we hide behind work that has no purpose?

Leader: I will rescue you from all the places to which you have been scattered on a day of clouds and thick darkness.

People: Will you nourish us, God, with food that restores our spirit?

Leader: I will feed you with justice.

People: Will you help us, God, to thrive beyond simple survival?

Leader: I will bind up the injured, and I will strengthen the weak. I will save my flock ... and I, the Lord, will be your God.

Collect

We rejoice, O God, that Christ is sovereign. We rejoice that we are a found people, no longer lost and no longer wandering alone through the wilderness. Praise be to our freeing Christ. Amen.

Prayer Of Confession

We know about days of clouds and thick darkness, O God, when we no longer can find our way. We are grateful for your promise to seek us out and shepherd us through such urgent times. In the name of Christ. Amen.

64A Hymns

"Rejoice, [Ye][You] Pure In Heart" Tune: MARION

"Such Perfect Love My Shepherd Shows" Tune: DOMINUS REGIT ME

"The King Of Love My Shepherd Is" Tune: ST. COLUMBA

Proper 29 (Christ The King)
Sunday between November 20 and November 26 inclusive

Second Lesson: Ephesians 1:15-23
Theme: Spirit Of Wisdom

Call To Worship
May your eyes light up with hope. May you gain in inner sight. May God give you a spirit of wisdom as you come to know God. May this time of worship fill you with a sense of the greatness of the power of God.

Collect
You have called us to a great hope and to a great challenge, O God. You have made the church the body of Christ. All glory be to your holy name. Amen.

Prayer Of Confession
You surprise us, O God, in the ways you make yourself known to us. We become aware of your presence as we make decisions. Timely opportunities come to us leading us on toward a new, suitable course. Persons touch our lives at a meaningful time. You surprise us, O God, with your greatness and your power. We thank you. In the name of Christ. Amen.

64A Hymns
"God The Omnipotent" Tune: RUSSIAN HYMN
"Praise, My Soul, The King of Heaven" or "Praise With Joy The World's Creator" Tune: PRAISE MY SOUL
"Thine Is The Glory" Tune: JUDAS MACCABEUS

Proper 29 (Christ The King)
Sunday between November 20 and November 26 inclusive

Gospel: Matthew 25:31-46
Theme: To The Least

Call To Worship

Leader: Does Christ still have power today?
People: Are you here, Jesus, in the alcoholic?
Leader: Does Christ still have power today?
People: Are you here, Jesus, in the person depressed into inactivity?
Leader: Does Christ still have power today?
People: Are you here, Jesus, in the child whose parents are divorcing, in the person newly confirmed as HIV-positive, Jesus?
Leader: Does Christ still have power today?

Collect

We praise you, O God, whose healing energy persistently makes itself known in a troubled world. We see you in the small act that makes a significant difference in one person's life. We see you in the pivotal actions of leaders and nations who labor to make their world a better place. We praise you for keeping your promises through Jesus Christ. Amen.

Prayer Of Confession

We come, O God, both as the needy and as those who quietly proclaim by our actions to those in difficulty that Jesus' love prevails. When we ourselves face burdensome times, remind us that we are not powerless. In turn, quicken awareness of ourselves as vehicles of Christ's power. Through Jesus the Christ. Amen.

64A Hymns

"Jesus Shall Reign" Tune: DUKE STREET
"Sing Praise To God" Tune: MIT FREUDEN ZART
"Rejoice, [Give Thanks And Sing][The Lord Is King]" Tune: DARWALL'S 148TH

Pentecost 27 (Lutheran)

First Lesson: Jeremiah 26:1-6
Theme: They Might Listen

Call To Worship
Part of standing firm in our faith involves speaking out when what we have to say is unpopular. Part of standing firm in faith embraces waiting for others to be able to hear. Part of standing firm includes knowing some of our labors will blow away in the wind but others will achieve fruition. So we must be of good courage as we stand firm in the faith.

Collect
We thank you, O Bounteous God, for your persistence in standing firm in the hope that your people might listen to the truths you set forth. We thank you for your tenacity in cheering us on. Through Christ. Amen.

Prayer Of Confession
O God, many important words we speak remain unheard by those we want to hear them — our children, parents, teachers, friends, employers, lifemates. Do we waste our energy? We have little control over another's listening or changing from disastrous ways. Give us the strength to continue trying to reach them and the hope that they might listen. In the name of Christ. Amen.

65A Hymns
"God Is Working His Purpose Out" Tune: PURPOSE
"Blest Are The Pure In Heart" Tune: FRANCONIA
"Now Thank We All Our God" Tune: NUN DANKET

Pentecost 27 (Lutheran)

Second Lesson: 1 Thessalonians 3:7-13
Theme: Standing Firm

Call To Worship

Stand firm in the faith. Stand firm in *your* faith. May God restore what is lacking in your faith. May holiness strengthen your hearts through all distress. Come, now, and let us worship God in gratitude and in faith.

Collect

We are witnesses to the faith of our forefathers and foremothers, O God. We also applaud the efforts of present-day parents to keep alive the faith in times equally hostile to a life of faith. We come here in this place today to thank you, Holy Parent, for your continual restoration of our faith. Amen.

Prayer Of Confession

Leader: Stand firm.
People: We waver and whimper. We stumble and stutter.
Leader: Stand firm.
People: We become lazy, too busy, and hazy of intention.
Leader: Stand firm in the faith.
All: Amen.

65A Hymns

"Faith Of [Our Fathers][The Martyrs]" Tune: ST. CATHERINE
"All Glory Be To God On High" Tune: ALLEIN GOTT IN DER HÖH
"Ye Watchers And Ye Holy Ones" Tune: LASST UNS ERFREUEN

Pentecost 27 (Lutheran)

Gospel: Matthew 24:1-14
Theme: How Will We Know?

Call To Worship
You alone are holy, O God. You alone are worthy. You are perfect in power, in love, and in purity. We worship you and praise your holy name.

Collect
Creator, Redeemer, and Bringer of the Holy, with your help, we reaffirm our promise to follow you.   Amen.

Prayer Of Confession
Leader: Beware that no one leads you astray.

People: Rumors and gossip and hearsay threaten to lead us astray.

Leader: Beware that no one leads you astray.

People: Those looking for self-importance attempt to lead us astray.

Leader: Beware that no one leads you astray.

People: The money-hungry and power-craved try to lead us astray.

All: We hear the good news, Holy God, that those who endure to the end will know salvation.

65A Hymns
"Holy, Holy, Holy" Tune: NICAEA

"Blessed Jesus, At Thy Word" or "We Have Gathered, Jesus Dear"
    Tune: LIEBSTER JESU

"O God Of Strength" Tune: WELWYN

Reformation Sunday

First Lesson: Jeremiah 31:31-34
Theme: Reform

Call To Worship

Leader: Reform.
People: Improve.
Leader: Reform.
People: Change.
Leader: Reform.
People: Transform.
Leader: Reform.
People: Revise and reshape.

Collect

As our denominations find new unity in these new times, O God, we pray that the changes improve. Our hope is to stretch toward greater breadth and depth. Our aim is to know the might of your fortress in our lives. We lift our prayers to you this day for all who have led and all who bring our church into the new century. For the sake of Jesus the Christ. Amen.

Prayer Of Confession

New covenants are risky, O God. History teaches us that you stand by us through the transformations that bring us into a greater communion with you and with one another. Remind us, always, that there are as many ways to say "I love you, God" as there are expressions of your love for us. We are your people and you are our God. Amen.

66A Hymns

"A Mighty Fortress Is Our God" Tune: EIN' FESTE BURG
"Out Of The Depths I Cry To You" Tune: AUS TIEFER NOT
"Built On [A][The] Rock, The Church Doth Stand" Tune: KIRKEN
   DEN ER ET

Reformation Sunday

Second Lesson: Romans 3:19-28
Theme: By Faith

Call To Worship

This world identifies us by what we do. Our contemporaries assess us according to our accomplishments. We come to this place of worship from many occupations and a variety of doing. Cease your doing for a moment and direct your attention to your being — simply being. This is what God sees. If in this essential being dimension, you have faith in Jesus Christ, that is enough for God's grace. Come, let us rejoice and sing.

Collect

We know a great reformation through your grace, O God. We pray for help with our faith so that it will mature and endure beyond sporadic bursts of emotion. Amen.

Prayer Of Confession

Leader: Your faith in Jesus Christ will save you.
People: We all have sinned, O God.
Leader: Your faith in Jesus Christ will save you.
People: We have fallen short in our actions.
Leader: Your faith in Jesus Christ will save you.
People: We have made a mess of our lives.
All: Christ will save us. Praise be to God. Amen.

66A Hymns

"My Hope Is Built On Nothing Less" Tune: SOLID ROCK
"All My Hope [Is Firm][On God Is Founded]" Tune: MICHAEL
"[Savior][Saviour], Like A Shepherd Lead Us" Tune: BRADBURY

Reformation Sunday

Gospel: John 8:31-36
Theme: Free At Last

Call To Worship

Leader: The truth will make you free,
People: Not a dollar for an "A" grade.
Leader: The truth will make you free,
People: Not coercion to do the right thing.
Leader: The truth will make you free,
People: Not expected compliments or hoped for honors.
All: The truth will make us free.

Collect

If we are to be true disciples of Christ, O God, then we must continue to live according to the words of Jesus beyond Sunday worship, beyond the observation of others whom we care about, and beyond the untruths our minds invent. We would know the freedom of truth and the truth of freedom. For the sake of Christ. Amen.

Prayer Of Confession

The smallest lie holds us in bondage. A dishonest thought enslaves our integrity. However camouflaged its name, sin imprisons us, O God, separating us from you, our neighbors, and ourselves. We are grateful for the possibility of reunion within the family of God through Jesus Christ. Amen.

66A Hymns

"I Know That My Redeemer [Lives][Liveth]" Tune: HANNAH
"We Shall Overcome" Tune: WE SHALL OVERCOME
"I'll Go Where You Want Me to Go" Tune: I'LL GO

All Saints' Sunday

First Lesson: Revelation 7:9-17
Theme: Salvation. Amen.

Call To Worship

Leader: The good news, the first word, is not of being condemned but of being saved.

People: "Amen! Blessing and glory and wisdom and thanksgiving and honor and power and might be to our God forever and ever! Amen."

Leader: You will hunger no more. You will thirst no more. Neither the sun nor the scorching heat will strike you.

People: "Amen! Blessing and glory and wisdom and thanksgiving and honor and power and might be to our God forever and ever! Amen."

Leader: For the Lamb of God will be your shepherd. He will guide you to springs of the water of life. God will wipe away every tear from your eyes.

People: "Amen! Blessing and glory and wisdom and thanksgiving and honor and power and might be to our God forever and ever! Amen."

All: So be it. Amen.

Collect

On this day of all saints, we praise you, dear God, and thank you for holding out to us the promise of everlasting life. We thank you for the images and metaphors of our faith that make tangible the hope that abides within our hearts. Amen.

Prayer Of Confession

We have something to look forward to. Precisely what its shape will be, we cannot know now. We have wonder-filled imaginings. We have dreams. So why do we worry about what comes after life here? Teach us again, Compassionate God, that just as we can trust ourselves to your care in this life, so can we trust your nearness in the next. Because of the Lamb of God, Jesus, our Savior. Amen.

67A Hymns

"Amen, Amen" Tune: AMEN

"O Mighty God, When I Survey In Wonder" Tune: O STORE GUD
   OR "How Great Thou Art" Tune: HOW GREAT THOU ART

"Faith Of The Martyrs" Tune: ST. CATHERINE

All Saints' Sunday

Second Lesson: 1 John 3:1-3
Theme: God's Children

Call To Worship

We come to this place of worship on this day of paying respect to the saints who have preceded us. We remember that they, too, were children of God. As children of God, we all belong to God. Praise be to God, the source of all who have been, who are, and who will be.

Collect

We praise you, O God, the power, the might, and the rock bolstering all who try to be Christian. We would be more holy. We would be more loving. We would be more like Jesus in our hearts. Amen.

Prayer Of Confession

We pray this day that you continue to strengthen us and that we might persist in fortifying one another along our life journeys. We know you do not call us to achieve perfection, Gracious God. You ask only that we do our best. When we stumble, you ask only that we try again. So let us be brave in our faith and in our deeds. For the sake of Jesus the Christ. Amen.

67A Hymns

"Of The [Father's Love] [Parent's Heart] Begotten" Tune: DIVINUM MYSTERIUM

"Lord, I Want To Be A Christian" Tune: I WANT TO BE A CHRISTIAN

"For All The Saints" Tune: SINE NOMINE or SARUM

All Saints' Sunday

Gospel: Matthew 5:1-12
Theme: Keep Trying

Call To Worship

Leader: What's in a name? What does hearing your name summon to mind?
People: The way we greet life,
Leader: Things we have accomplished,
People: Personal uniqueness,
Leader: Hopes and plans others have had for us.
People: What's in your name?
All: The whisper of God's blessing.

Collect

We lift up to you this day of all saints, Gracious God, those we know, have known, and whom we have heard about who have kept trying despite derision, unpopularity, or adverse circumstance. We are grateful for their lives and for the difference they have brought to our lives. Through the name of Jesus the Christ. Amen.

Prayer Of Confession

There are times, O God, when we catch ourselves being saints. Yes, saints. No, we are not bragging. These are the pure times of sharing of ourselves without thought of self, gaining something in return, or even receiving your blessing. They may be only moments or just a thought, but when they happen, we feel close to you. We feel whole and fully whom you mean for us to be. Thank you, Holy One, for the times we brush sainthood. Amen.

67A Hymns

"I Sing A Song Of The Saints Of God"[1] Tune: GRAND ISLE
"Blessed Are The Poor In Spirit" Tune: ANNIKA'S DANCE **OR** "Ten
    Thousand Times Ten Thousand" Tune: ALFORD
"Shall We Gather At The River" Tune: HANSON PLACE

---

1. Between verses, invite the calling out of names of saints or mentors in the lives of those in the congregation.

Day Of Thanksgiving

First Lesson: Deuteronomy 8:7-18
Theme: Every Living Thing

Call To Worship

We have come to express our indebtedness to God, the giver of abundant and bountiful gifts. We speak on behalf of a land and a people grateful for efforts of human care. Come, let us give thanks to God.

Collect

Hear the prayers this day of a thankful people and a grateful world, O Thou Sustaining and Nurturing Parent of all. Amen.

Prayer Of Confession

Leader: To those who set out yarn scraps and dryer lint last spring and suet for the winter, the nesting birds and the overwintering birds say thanks.

People: For those who spread over them a load of dried farmyard manure and for those who collected and offered nutrient-sweet, rain barrel water, the flower gardens and vegetable patches say thanks.

Leader: For those who recycled usable articles of clothing, wearers know a sense of pride at looking nice and feel gratitude for staying warm.

People: For those who shared with food banks items from their bounty, recipients confess their gratitude for food in their stomachs and in the tummies of their children, enabling them to work and learn with more energy and to want to keep trying.

Leader: For all who decided not to burn trash and to all who planted a tree this year, the air we breathe is grateful.

People: For you who minimized or eliminated the use of pesticides and herbicides and who refused to pour old motor oil on the land, the earth is grateful.

All: To all who, rather than bury reusable resources in dead-end landfills, have cared enough about the earth to choose to continue recycling, we offer this prayer of affirmation. Amen.

210

68A Hymns

"We [Plough][Plow] The Fields And Scatter" Tune: WIR PFLUGEN
OR "Touch The Earth Lightly" Tune: TENDERNESS
"All Things Bright And Beautiful" Tune: ROYAL OAK
"My God, I Thank Thee, Who Hast Made" Tune: WENTWORTH

Day Of Thanksgiving

Second Lesson: 2 Corinthians 9:6-15
Theme: Thank You

Call To Worship

Girls and Women: For providing us with enough that we might share with others,

All: **We thank you, O Generous God.**

Boys and Men: For supplying the world with persons capable of meticulous medical research,

All: **We thank you, O Generous God.**

Girls and Women: For endowing our hearts with qualities of peace, trust, and aspiration,

All: **We thank you, O Generous God.**

Boys and Men: For giving your Son for our redemption,

All: **We thank you, O Generous God. Amen.**

Collect

Our hearts overflow with thanksgivings to you, O Bountiful Creator. Let the collected prayers of all who worship this hour of thanksgiving sing a vigorous chorus of praise to you. In the name of Jesus the Christ. Amen.

Prayer Of Confession

God grant that we might extend our gratitude beyond this day. God grant that we might stretch our generosity beyond immediate families. God grant that we might channel the skills and talents you have given us toward healing action in our world. Amen.

68A Hymns

"We Praise [Thee][You], O God" Tune: KREMSER

"God Of The Sparrow, God Of The Whale" Tune: ROEDER **OR** "Praise To God, Immortal Praise" Tune: DIX

"For The Fruit[s] Of [All][This] Creation" Tune: AR HYD Y NOS or EAST ACKLAM

Day Of Thanksgiving

Gospel: Luke 17:11-19
Theme: Gratitude

Call To Worship

Leader: Come, let us give thanks to the one who said, "Get up and go on your way; your faith has made you well."

People: We give thanks to you, O Christ.

Collect

Restorer of the will to live, Healer of emotional pain, Mender of broken hearts, Calmer of physical suffering, and Quieter of grief, to you we lift our hearts in praise. Amen.

Prayer Of Confession

We forget, O God, how many ways you bring healing. At times our suffering is so intense that when we find a bit of relief, we hurry back to what we want to do. We forget to stand still and give you thanks for the healing. We pause to thank you for the grace of healing which frees us to live more fully. Amen.

68A Hymns

"We Gather Together" Tune: KREMSER
"What Gift Can We Bring?" Tune: ANNIVERSARY SONG
"[O][Our] God, Our Help In Ages Past" Tune: ST. ANNE

Index Of Hymns

GG   = *God's Glory: Hymns by Dosia Carlson* (The Beatitudes Center for Developing Older Adult Resources: 555 W. Glendale Avenue, Phoenix AZ 85201) (Carlson is UCC)
LCA   = *Service Book and Hymnal of the Lutheran Church In America*
MSL   = Missouri Synod Lutheran
NCH   = *New Century Hymnal* (United Church of Christ)
PH   = *Pilgrim Hymnal* (UCC)
PRH   = *The Hymnal For Worship and Celebration* (Presbyterian)
TSH   = *The Service Hymnal* (Chicago, IL: Hope Publishing Company)
UMH   = *United Methodist Hymnal*
WJOSS = *With Joy Our Spirits Sing: The Hymns of Rae E. Whitney* (Kingston, NY: Selah Pub. Co. (Whitney is an Episcopalian)

TUNE	TITLE	HYMNAL(S)	CODE IN TEXT
A			
ABBOT'S LEIGH	God Is Here	NCH, UMH	49A
ABERYSTWYTH	Watcher, Tell Us Of	NCH	01A
"	Watchman, Tell Us	LCA, NCH, PH, PRH	01A
ACCEPTANCE	Help Us Accept Each	UMH	52A
ACKLEY	He Lives	PRH, UMH	28A, 40A
ADELAIDE	Have Thine Own Way	UMH, PRH	19A, 54A
ADESTE FIDELIS	How Firm A Founda	LCA, MSL, NCH, PH, PRH	46A
"	[O][Oh] Come, All Y	LCA, MSL, NCH, PH, PRH, UMH	04A
ADORO TE	Here, O My Lord, I	LCA, MSL, NCH, PH, PRH, UMH	38A
AFRICAN A	Every Time I Feel	NCH, UMH	46A
ALFORD	Ten Thousand Times	LCA, PH	67A
ALLEIN GOTT	All Glory Be To God	LCA, MSL, PH	37A, 65A
AMAZING GRAC	Amazing Grace, How	MSL, NCH, PRH, UMH	11A, 53A
AMEN	Amen, Amen	NCH	08A, 27A, 67A
ANCIENT OF D	Hope Of The World	LCA, NCH	41A
ANGEL'S STOR	O Jesus, I Have Pr	LCA, NCH, PH, PRH, UMH	11A, 39A, 62A
ANNIKA'S DAN	Blessed Are The Po	NCH	12A, 48A, 67A
ANNIVERSARY	What Gift Can We B	NCH, UMH	68A
ANTIOCH	Joy To The World	LCA, MSL, NCH, PH, PRH, UMH	04A, 05A
AR HYD Y NOS	For The Fruit	NCH, UMH	68A
"	Go, My Children, Wi	NCH, UMH	44A, 48A
"	God Who Madest Ear	LCA, MSL, PH, UMH	47A
ARMENIA	All Praise To Our	PRH, UMH	58A
ARNSBERG	God [Himself][Is]	LCA, MSL, NCH, PH	10A, 29A, 59A
ARTHUR'S SEA	March On, O Soul, Wi	PH	24A
ASSURANCE	Blessed Assurance	NCH, PRH, UMH	33A, 50A

AURELIA	Help Us Accept Each	NCH	52A
"	The Church's One Fou	LCA, MSL, NCH, PH, PRH, UMH	15A
AUS TIEFER N	Out Of The Depths I	LCA, UMH	66A
AUSTRIAN	Glorious Things Of	LCA, MSL, NCH, PH, PRH, UMH	43A, 60A
"	God, Whose Giving Kn	NCH	60A
"	Lord, We Thank Thee	PH	52A
"	Not Alone For Might	LCA, PH	42A
AWAY IN A	Away In a Manger	LCA, MSL, NCH, PH, PRH, UMH	04A
AZMON	Come, Let Us Join	NCH	21A
"	[O][Oh] For A Thous	MSL, NCH, UMH	50A, 62A
"	O For A World	NCH	14A

B

BALM IN GILEAD	There Is A Balm	UMH	48A
BANGOR	I Know Not How	PH	09A, 50A
BATTLE HYMN	[My] Mine Eyes Hav	LCA, NCH, PH, PRH, UMH	63A
BEACH SPRING	As We Gather At Yo	NCH	58A
"	Sunday's Palms Are	WJOSS	19A
BEACON HILL	Are Ye Able	UMH	41A
BEATITUDO	Immortal Love, For	NCH, PH	40A, 49A
"	O For A Closer Bon	NCH	62A
BEECHER	Called As Partners	NCH	15A
"	Love Divine, All Lov	LCA, MSL, NCH, PH, PRH, UMH	07A, 35A, 61A
BEGINNINGS	This Is A Day Of New	NCH, UMH	07A, 08A, 15A, 42A
BENJAMIN	Spirit Of Jesus, If	NCH	54A
BETHANY	Nearer, My God, To	LCA, MSL, NCH, PH, UMH	22A, 33A
BISHOPGAR	Who Trusts In God A	MSL, PH	49A, 63A
BISHOPTHOR	How Lovely Are Thy	PH	31A
"	How Lovely Is Your	NCH	31A
BLESSED QU	Joys Are Flowing Li	NCH	33A
BLESSINGS	Count Your Blessings	PRH, TSH	48A
BONHOEFFER	By Gracious Powers	NCH	47A
BOYLSTON	Blessed [Blest] Be T	LCA, NCH, PH, UMH	20A
BRADBURY	Savio[u]r, Like A Sh	LCA, NCH, PH, PRH, UMH	31A, 66A
BREAD OF LI	Break [Now][Thou]	LCA, NCH, PH, PRH, UMH	38A, 48A
BROTHER JAME	God Is My Shepherd	NCH	31A
BUNESSAN	Living With Birthing	GG	21A, 37A
"	Morning Has Broken	PH, PRH, UMH	37A
BY AND BY	We Are Often Tosse	NCH	47A
"	We'll Understand I	PRH, UMH	47A

C

CANONBURY	[God][Lord], Speak	LCA, NCH, PH, PRH, UMH	18A, 47A, 50A
"	We Want To Learn To	GG	22A, 45A
CANTERBURY	Depth Of Mercy	UMH	58A
"	Holy Spirit, [Light	MSL	16A
"	Holy Spirit, [Truth	LCA, NCH, PH, UMH	16A
CAROL	It Came Upon A Mid	LCA, MSL, NCH, PH, PRH, UMH	03A, 04A
CENACLE	In The Silence	GG	23A
CHEREPONI	Jesu, Jesu, Fill U	NCH, UMH	48A
CHRISTE SANC	Christ Is The World	UMH	34A
"	Father, We Praise T	LCA, MSL, NCH, PH, UMH	30A
CHRISTMAS	Awake, My Soul, Str	LCA, NCH, PH	59A
CHTMAS SONG	There's A Song In	UMH	03A, 06A
CHRISTPRAIS	O Praise The Graci	NCH	45A
CLOISTERS	Lord Of Our Life, A	LCA, MSL, PH	51A
COMPASSION	We Are Pilgrims On	GG	20A
CONDITOR	Creator Of The Stars	NCH, PH, UMH	01A
CONSOLATION	Still, Still With	LCA, PH	62A
CONSOLATOR	Come, Ye Disconso	LCA, PRH, UMH	41A
CORONATION	All Hail The Power	MSL, NCH, PH, PRH, UMH	09A, 34A
CRANHAM	In The Bleak Midwin	LCA, NCH, PH, UMH	03A
CRAVEN	When, Like The Woma	NCH	22A
CRIMOND	The Lord's My Shep	LCA, MSL, PH, PRH, UMH	31A
CUSHMAN	We Would See Jesus,	PH, UMH	10A, 42A
CWM RHONDDA	For The Healing	NCH, UMH	57A
"	God Of Grace And Go	MSL, NCH, PH, PRH, UMH	45A, 49A
"	Guide Me, O My [Tho	LCA, MSL, NCH, PH, PRH, UMH	40A

D

DARWALL'S 1	Rejoice, Give Thank	NCH	64A
"	Rejoice, The Lord I	PH, PRH, UMH	64A
DENNIS	Blessed [Blest] Be	NCH, PH, UMH	20A, 41A
"	How Gentle God's Co	PH	16A
DIADEMATA	And Have You Never	WJOSS	50A
"	Crown Him With Many	LCA, MSL, PH, PRH, UMH	36A
"	Crown With Your Ric	NCH	36A
"	Maker, In Whom We L	UMH	54A
"	Praise To The Living	NCH	54A, 57A
DIFFERENT S	Sing A Different Song	NCH	06A
DIVINUM MYS	Of The Father's Lov	LCA, MSL, PH, PRH, UMH	08A, 67A
"	Of The Parent's Hea	NCH	08A, 67A

DIX	As With Gladness	LCA, MSL, NCH, PH, PRH	08A
"	For The Beauty Of	LCA, NCH, PH, PRH, UMH	14A, 29A, 50A
"	Praise To God, Immo	MSL, PH	68A
DOMINUS REG	Such Perfect Love M	NCH	64A
DONNE SECOU	Father, In Thy Myst	PH	63A
"	Hope Of The World	PH	41A
DOWN AMPNEY	Come [Forth][Down]	LCA, NCH, PH, UMH	15A
DULCE CARME	Lead Us, Heavenly F	PH	42A
DUKE STREET	Forth In [Thy][Your	LCA, MSL, PH, UMH	24A, 64A
"	Jesus Shall Reign	LCA, MSL, NCH, PH, PRH, UMH	34A, 48A
"	O God, Beneath Thy	PH	44A
DUNDEE	God Moves In A Myst	LCA, MSL, NCH, PH, PRH	47A
"	I To The Hills Will	PH	56A
DUNLAP'S CR	We Live By Faith An	NCH	34A
DURROW	O God Thou Art The	PH	37A

E

EAST ACKLAM	For The Fruits Of	UMH	68A
EASTER HYMN	Christ The Lord Is	LCA, MSL, NCH, PH, PRH, UMH	28A
EBENEZER	Come, O Spirit, Dwe	NCH	36A
"	God Hath Spoken By	UMH	36A
"	Once To Every Man	LCA, PH, PRH	09A, 45A
EIN' FESTE	A Mighty Fortress	LCA, MSL, NCH, PH, PRH, UMH	22A, 66A
ELLACOMBE	Hosanna, Loud Hosan	MSL, NCH, PH, PRH, UMH	25A
"	I Sing The Mighty P	NCH, PH	12A, 33A, 54A
"	We Hail You God's A	NCH	03A
"	We Sing The Almight	MSL	33A, 54A
"	With Songs And Hon	PH	62A
ELLERS	Not As The World Gi	WJOSS	32A
"	Savior, Again To [Th	LCA, MSL, NCH, PH, PRH, UMH	40A
"	Take Up The Song	WJOSS	36A
ELTON	Let There Be Light	PH, NCH	13A, 34A
EMMAUS	On The Day Of Resurr	UMH	28A
ENDLESS SO	My Life Flows On In	NCH	31A
ERIE	What A Friend We	LCA, MSL, NCH, PH, PRH	44A
ERMUNTRE DI	Break Forth, O Beau	LCA, NCH, PH, PRH, UMH	03A
ES IST EIN	Lo, How A Rose	LCA, MSL, NCH, PH, PRH, UMH	02A
EUCHARISTI	Bread Of The W	LCA, NCH, PH, UMH	26A, 38A

218

FAITHFULNESS	Great Is [Your][Th	NCH, UMH	10A, 31A, 55A
FEDERAL STR	Jesus, Where'er Thy	PH	59A
FENNVILLE	Out Of The Depths,	NCH	26A
FESTAL SONG	Arise, Your Light I	NCH	08A, 13A
"	Rise Up, O Church O	PRH	13A, 53A
"	Rise Up, O Men Of G	LCA, PH, UMH	13A, 53A
FFIGYSBREN	O Thou Great Friend	PH	53A
FINLANDIA	Be [Calm][Still], M	LCA, MSL, NCH, PH, PRH, UMH	16A, 42A
"	We Would Be Buildin	NCH, PH	32A, 47A
FINLAY	O Be Joyful In The	PH	16A
FOREST GREEN	[I][We] Sing The	NCH, PH, UMH	54A
"	Now Bless The God O	NCH	11A
"	O Spirit Of The Liv	LCA, NCH, UMH	58A
FOUNDATION	How Firm A Founda	NCH, PH, UMH	46A
FRANCONIA	Blest Are The Pure	LCA, PH	12A, 64A

GALILEE	Jesus Calls Us O'er	LCA, NCH, PH, PRH, UMH	15A, 52A
GENEVA 124	Go Forth For God	UMH	41A
GERMANY	Where Cross The Cr	LCA, NCH, PH, UMH	52A
GIFT OF LOVE	The Gift Of Love	UMH	56A
GLORIA	Angels We Have Hea	LCA, MSL, NCH, PH, PRH, UMH	04A
GO DOWN, MOS	When Israel Was In	NCH, PH, UMH	22A
GO TELL IT	Go Tell It On The M	MSL, NCH, PH, PRH, UMH	06A
GOD BE WITH	God Be With You	NCH, PH, PRH, UMH	53A
GOTTLOB, ES	God Of The Living, I	PH	29A
GRAND ISLE	I Sing A Song Of Th	NCH, PH, UMH	67A
GREENSLEEVES	What Child Is This	LCA, MSL, NCH, PH, PRH, UMH	05A
GROSSER GOT	Holy God, We Praise	PH, NCH, UMH	46A
GUIDE MY FE	Guide My Feet	NCH	49A, 62A
GWALCHMAI	Glory Be To God On	PH	60A

HAMBURG	When I Survey The	LCA, MSL, NCH, PH, PRH, UMH	23A
HANKEY	I Love To Tell The	LCA, NCH, UMH	18A
HANNAH	I Know That My Re	PRH, LCA, MSL	66A
HANOVER	[Ye][You] Servants	LCA, NCH, PH, PRH, UMH	35A, 61A
HANSON PLACE	Shall We Gather At	NCH, UMH	67A
HARTFORD	To Christ We Turn	GG	21A
"	Victory In Jesus	PRH, UMH	21A

HAYDN	Wake, My Soul	NCH	24A
HE LEADETH	He Leadeth Me	LCA, PH, PRH, UMH	55A
HEINLEIN	Forty Days And Fo	NCH, PH	20A
HERE I AM,	Here I Am, Lord	UMH	43A
HERMON	We Bear The Strain	PH	47A
HERR JESU C	God Of The Earth,	PH	47A
HERZLIEBSTE	Ah, Holy Jesus	LCA, NCH, PH, UMH	25A, 27A
HESPERUS	Father In Heaven,	PH	19A
"	Jesus [Thou][The]	NCH, PH	38A
"	O God Of Love, O G	LCA, MSL, NCH, PH	13A
"	O Grant Us Light	NCH	34A
HOLINESS	Take Time To Be Hol	PRH, TSH, UMH	20A, 58A
HOLY MANNA	God, We Thank You	NCH	60A
"	God Who Stretched	NCH, UMH	60A
"	Take My Gifts	NCH	43A, 60A
HOW GREAT	How Great Thou Art	MSL, PRH, UMH	28A, 67A
HUMMEL	God's Glory Is A W	PH	53A
HURSLEY	Dear Jesus, In Who	UMH	55A
HYFRYDOL	Alleluia! All	LCA, NCH	50A
"	God Of Earth And Se	PH	12A
"	God The Spirit, Gu	UMH	18A
"	Let Us Hope When	NCH	41A
"	Praise The Lord, Y	LCA, PH, PRH	18A, 54A
"	We Have Come At Ch	NCH	18A
HYMN TO JOY	Joyful, Joyful We	LCA, NCH, PH, PRH, UMH	07A, 46A
"	O How Glorious, Fu	NCH, PH	63A

I

I AM THINE	I Am Yours [Thine]	NCH, PRH, UMH	21A, 43A
I WANT TO B	Lord, I Want To B	NCH, PH, UMH	11A, 25A, 38A, 66A
I WONDER AS	I Wonder As I Wander	PRH	26A
I'LL GO	I'll Go Where You	PRH	65A
ICH HALTE T	And Have You Ne	WJOSS	50A
"	Give To The Winds	NCH, PH, UMH	21A, 35A
"	Give Up Your Anxi	NCH	21A, 35A, 57A
ID Y ENSEÑA	Sois la Semilla	NCH, UMH	46A
"	You Are The Seed	NCH, UMH	46A
IDA	Christ Will Come A	NCH	46A
IN BABILONE	O How Glorious, Fu	NCH, PH	63A
"	There's A Wideness	LCA, NCH, PH, PRH	41A
IN DIR IST	In [Thee][You] Is Gl	MSL, UMH	28A
IN DULCI JU	Good Christian [Fri	LCA, MSL, NCH, PH, PRH, UMH	06A
INNOCENTS	As The Sun Doth Da	UMH	10A
"	Christian, Rise An	NCH, PH	43A, 57A
"	Let Us All With Gl	MSL	10A, 61A
"	Let Us With A Glad	LCA, NCH, PH	10A, 61A

INTEGER VIT	Father Almighty, B	NCH, PH	50A
INTERCESSOR	By Gracious Powers	UMH	47A
"	Children Of God	NCH	39A, 59A
"	O Brother Man, Fol	LCA, PH	39A, 59A
ISTE CONFES	Lord Of Our Life, A	LCA, MSL, PH	51A
ITALIAN HY	Come, [Now][Thou] A	LCA, MSL, NCH, PH, PRH, UMH	56A
IVERSON	Spirit Of The Livi	NCH, PRH	13A, 40A

J

JACOB'S LAD	We Are Climbing Ja	NCH, PH, UMH	48A
"	We Are Dancing Sar	NCH	48A
JEFFERSON	God Our Author A	NCH	41A
JESU, MEIN	[Jesu][Jesus], Price	LCA, MSL, NCH, PH, PRH, UMH	30A
JESUS LOVES	Jesus Loves Me	NCH, PRH, UMH	57A
JOSEPH LIEB	Gentle Joseph, Jos	NCH	04A
JUDAS MACCA	Sing To The Lord A	GG	28A
"	Thine Is The Glory	LCA, NCH, PH, PRH, UMH	28A, 64A

K

KARED ABOUT	We Are The Cared A	GG	19A
KATHERINE	God Of Change And	NCH, UMH	36A
KEDRON	Creating God, Your	UMH	59A
KENTRIDGE	O Christ, The Healer	NCH	40A
KING'S WEST	At The Name Of Jesus	LCA, MSL, PH, PRH, UMH	34A
KINGS OF OR	We Three Kings	PH, UMH	08A
KINGSFOLD	O Master Workman Of	PH	39A
KIRKEN DEN	Built On [A][The] Ro	LCA, MSL, PH	39A, 66A
KREMSER	Thus Far You Have Le	GG	16A
"	We Gather Together	PRH, UMH	53A, 68A
"	We Praise [Thee][You	LCA, NCH, PH, PRH	68A

L

LAKE ENON	Jesus, I Live To You	NCH	55A
LANCASHIRE	In Egypt Under Phar	NCH	51A
"	Lead On Eternal Sov	NCH	13A, 45A
"	Lead On O King Eter	LCA, PH, PRH, UMH	13A, 45A
"	The Day Of Resurrect	LCA, MSL, NCH, PH, PRH, UMH	29A
LAND OF RE	Lord, Who Throughout	NCH, PH, UMH	19A
LANGHAM	Father Eternal, Rul	PH	54A
LANGRAN	Here, O My Lord, I	LCA, MSL, PH, PRH, UMH	59A
"	Lead Us, O Father	PH	10A

LASST UNS	All Creatures Of Our	MSL, NCH, PH, PRH, UMH	34A
"	Ye Watchers And Ye	MSL, LCA, PH, UMH	11A, 65A
LATTIMER	This Little Light Of	NCH, UMH	13A
LAUDA ANIMA	God, Whose Love Is	UMH	29A, 59A
LAUDES DOMI	Let Every Christian	NCH	36A
"	When Morning Gilds	LCA, MSL, NCH, PH, PRH, UMH	14A, 53A
LEAD ME, LO	Lead Me, Lord	LCA, PH, PRH, UMH	55A
LEONI	The God Of Abraham	LCA, MSL, NCH, PH, PRH, UMH	18A, 58A
LET US BREAK	Let Us Break Bread	NCH, PH, PRH, UMH	26A
LET US HOPE	Let Us Hope When	NCH	41A
LIEBSTER JE	Blessed Jesus, At	MSL, PH, UMH	35A, 65A
"	We Have Gathered,	NCH	65A
LITTLE BABY	See The Little Baby	NCH	05A
LLANFAIR	Praise The Lord, His	PH	29A
LLANGLOFFAN	O God Of Earth And A	LCA, NCH, PH	12A, 63A
"	O God Of Every Natio	UMH	12A
LLANHERNE	Angels Holy, High A	PH	07A
LLANLLYFNI	Make Me A Captive	LCA, PH	42A, 60A
LLANSANNAN	God Of Earth And Se	PH	12A
LOBE DEN HE	Praise To The Lord	LCA, MSL, PH, PRH, UMH	13A, 34A, 56A
"	Sing Praise To God	LCA, MSL, NCH, PRH	13A, 34A
LOBT GOTT	O Gracious God, Whos	PH	33A
LONGSTAFF	Take Time to Be Holy	PRH, TSH	20A
LORD, MAKE	Lord, Make Me More	NCH	19A
LORD OF THE	Lord Of The Dance	UMH	38A
LOUVAN	Lord Of All Being,	LCA, PH	54A
LUX BENIGN	Lead, Kindly Light	LCA, PH	62A
LYONS	[O][Oh] Worship The	LCA, MSL, PH, PRH, UMH	10A, 57A
"	We Worship You, God	NCH	10A, 57A
LYTLINGTON	God Be In My Head	PH	18A, 45A

M

MAPLE	Be Still And Know Th	GG	33A
MARION	Rejoice, [Ye][You]	LCA, NCH, PH, UMH	14A, 30A, 64A
MARTIN	Be Not Dismayed	NCH, PRH, UMH	16A, 33A, 55A
"	God Will Take Care	NCH, PRH, UMH	16A, 33A, 55A
MARYTON	O [Master][Savior]	LCA, NCH, PH, PRH, UMH	63A
MATERNA	How Beautiful, Our	NCH	52A
"	O Beautiful, For	LCA, PH, PRH, UMH	52A
MAUNDY THU	Christ At Table T	NCH	26A
McAFEE	Near to the Heart	PRH, UMH	41A

222

McKEE	In Christ There Is	NCH, PH, PRH, UMH	55A
MEDITATION	There Is A Green Hi	LCA, PH	20A
MEIN LEBEN	God Is My Strong Sal	PH	31A
MEINE HOFFN	All My Hope On God	PH	52A
MEIRIONYDD	O Come To Me, You	NCH	44A
"	The Voice Of God Is	PH, UMH	21A, 44A, 51A
MELCOMBE	New Every Morning	PH, UMH	46A
"	O Spirit Of The Liv	LCA, NCH, PH	58A
MELITA	Eternal Father,	LCA, PH, PRH	62A
MELROSE	God Send Us Men Wh	PH	44A
MENDELSSOHN	Hark The Herald Ang	LCA, MSL, NCH, PH, PRH, UMH	02A
MENDON	Come, Gracious Spir	LCA, MSL, PH	10A
MERCY	Holy Spirit, Truth	LCA, NCH, PH	24A, 36A, 55A
MESSIAH	Take My Life And Le	LCA, MSL, PH, PRH, UMH	56A
MICHAEL	All My Hope Is Firm	UMH	30A, 66A
"	All My Hope On God	NCH	30A, 66A
MILES LANE	All Hail The Power	MSL, NCH, PH, PRH, UMH	09A, 34A
MIT FREU	All Glory be To God	MSL, PH	30A
"	Sing Praise To God	NCH, PH, UMH	29A, 64A
MONKLAND	Praise, O Praise	PH	59A
MORE LOVE T	More Love To Thee	LCA, PH, PRH, UMH	15A, 57A
"	More Love To You	NCH	15A
MORECAMBE	Spirit Of God Desce	LCA, NCH, PH, PRH, UMH	08A, 46A
MORNING HYM	Awake, My Soul And	MSL, PH	14A, 42A
"	Forth In [Thy][Your]	LCA, MSL, PH, UMH	24A, 61A
MORNING SON	My Master, See, The	UMH	11A
MORNINGTON	Teach Me, My God	LCA, PH	15A, 63A
MUNICH	O Word Of God Incar	LCA, MSL, NCH, PH, PRH, UMH	39A, 61A

N

NATIONAL HY	God Of Our Fathers	LCA, MSL, PH, PRH	56A
"	God Of The Ages, Wh	NCH, UMH	56A
NEAR THE CR	Jesus, Keep Me Nea	NCH, PRH, UMH	22A
NEED	I Need Thee Every H	LCA, NCH, PH, PRH, UMH	49A
NETTLETON	Come, O Fount of Ev	NCH, UMH	21A
NEUMARK	If [You][Thou] But	LCA, MSL, NCH, PH, UMH	14A, 45A, 54A
NEW HOPE	Jesus Took The Brea	NCH	26A
NEW REFORM	God, Creation's Gre	NCH	32A
NICAEA	Holy, Holy, Holy	LCA, MSL, NCH, PH, PRH, UMH	15A, 37A, 65A

NUN DANKET	Now Thank We All	LCA, MSL, NCH, PH, PRH, UMH	11A, 65A
"	Spirit Divine, Atten	PH	31A
"	Spirit Divine, Hear	PRH	31A
NUN FREUT	We Come Unto Our Fa	PH	30A
NYLAND	In Heavenly Love Ab	LCA, PH, PRH	25A

O

O GOTT, DU	Christ Is The World's	PH, UMH	34A
O HOW I LO	O How I Love Jesus	PRH, UMH	56A
"	There Is A Name I	NCH, PRH, UMH	56A
O JESU CHRI	Dear Master, In Whos	PH	55A
O STORE GUD	O Mighty God, When	NCH	67A
O WALY WALY	When Love Is Found	NCH	44A
OHIO	We Can Be Hope	GG	33A
OLD 22ND	Thou God Of All, Wh	PH	57A
"	We Limit Not The Tr	NCH	57A
OLD HUNDR	All People That On	LCA, MSL, NCH, PH, PRH, UMH	07A, 35A, 38A
"	From All That Dwell	LCA, MSL, PH, UMH	30A, 38A
"	That King Before Wh	WJOSS	09A
OLIVET	My Faith Looks Up	LCA, MSL, PH, PRH, UMH	40A
OPEN MY E	Open My Eyes	UMH, PRH	20A, 46A
ORA LABORA	Come, Labor On	NCH, PH	53A
ORIENTIS P	Jesus, Our Brother,	NCH, UMH	06A
ORWIGSBURG	I Must Tell Jesus	NCH, PRH	31A

P

PACEM	A World Of Love And	GG	02A
PARK STREET	Before Jehovah's Aw	LCA, MSL, PH	53A
PASS IT ON	It Only Takes A Spa	UMH, PRH	24A, 49A
PASS ME NOT	Pass Me Not, O Gent	LCA, NCH, PRH, UMH	23A, 24A
PASSION CHO	O Sacred Head, Now	LCA, MSL, NCH, PH, PRH, UMH	22A, 27A
"	The King Shone In H	WJOSS	18A
"	To Love Just Those	WJOSS	58A
"	We Yearn, O [Chris	GG, NCH	01A, 22A, 44A
PEACE LIKE	I've Got Peace L	NCH, PRH	41A
PEACE, MY	Peace I Leave Wi	NCH	29A
PEEK	I Would Be True	NCH, PH	39A
PENITENT	It's Me, It's Me, O	UMH	20A, 35A
PENTECOST	Fight The Good Fight	LCA, MSL, PH	48A
"	Let There Be Light	PH, NCH	13A, 34A
PERSONENT H	On This Day Earth S	PH, UMH	06A
PICARDY	Let All Mortal Flesh	LCA, MSL, NCH, PH, UMH	01A

PILOT	Jesus, Savior, Pilo	LCA, MSL, NCH, PH, UMH	22A
PLEADING SAV	Jesus, Thou Divine	PH	43A, 60A
PORT JERVIS	We Are The Church	UMH	51A
POUCHER	Time Moves Forward	GG	24A
PRAISE MY S	Praise, My Soul,	LCA, PH, PRH, UMH	12A, 64A
"	Praise With Joy	NCH	64A
PRECIOUS LO	Precious Lord, Take	NCH, PRH, UMH	23A, 55A
PROCRASTINA	I'll Listen To Frie	GG	21A
PROMISE	In The Bulb There I	NCH	07A, 18A
"	Hymn Of Promise	UMH	07A, 18A
PSALM 42	Comfort, Comfort [O	LCA, MSL, NCH, PH	01A
PUER NOBIS	O Holy Spirit, Roo	NCH	45A
"	O Splendor Of God's	LCA, MSL, PH	01A
PURPOSE	God Is Working His	PH	07A, 47A, 65A

Q

QUEM PASTOR	Grant Us Wisdom To	NCH	58A

R

RAMWOLD	Creation's Lord, We	PH	08A, 37A
RATHBUN	In The Cross Of Ch	LCA, MSL, NCH, PH, PRH, UMH	11A, 60A
RATISBON	Christ, Whose Glory	LCA, PH, UMH	03A, 18A, 61A
REDHEAD NO.	Go [Journey] To Dar	LCA, MSL, NCH, PH, UMH	25A, 26A
"	Gracious Spirit, D	PH	36A
REGENSBURG	Father, Hear The Pr	PH	23A
REGENT SQUA	Angels From The Rea	LCA, MSL, NCH, PH, PRH, UMH	06A
"	Christ Is Made The	LCA, NCH, PH, PRH, UMH	15A, 32A, 57A
Response	Into My Heart, Lord	TSH	09A, 50A
RESURRECT	Because He Lives	PRH, UMH	28A
REST	Dear God, Embracing	NCH	44A
"	Dear Lord And Fathe	LCA, PH, PRH, UMH	44A
RHOSYMEDRE	My Song Is Love	LCA, MSL, NCH, PH	43A, 57A
RHUDDLAN	Judge Eternal, Thro	LCA, PH	44A
RICHMOND	O For A Heart To Pr	UMH	62A
RINGE RECHT	Lord, Thy Mercy Now	PH	52A
ROCK OF AGE	O Be Joyful In The	PH	16A, 52A
ROCKINGHAM	Incarnate God, Imm	NCH	14A, 18A, 51A
"	Strong Son Of God,	PH	14A, 18A, 51A
ROCKPORT	Hail To The Lord's	LCA, MSL, PH	51A
ROEDER	God Of The Sparrow,	NCH, UMH	28A, 67A
ROLLINGBAY	May The Sending One	NCH	56A
ROYAL OAK	All Things Bright A	NCH, PH, PRH, UMH	68A

225

RUSSIAN HYM	Christ The Victorio	UMH	12A
"	God The Omnipotent	LCA, NCH, PH, PRH	12A, 64A

S

ST. AGNES	Come, Holy Spirit,	MSL, NCH, PH, PRH	10A, 37A
"	Jesus, the Very Tho	LCA, NCH, PH, PRH, UMH	29A
"	Jesus, United By Th	UMH	10A
"	O Lord And Master O	PH	61A
"	Prayer Is The Soul'	LCA, NCH, UMH	47A
ST. ANDREW	Jesus Calls Us O'er	LCA, NCH, PH	52A
ST. ANNE	Creator God, Creati	NCH	37A
"	[O][Our] God, Our He	LCA, MSL, NCH, PH, UMH	23A, 68A
ST. ASAPH	Through The Night O	LCA, PH	53A
ST. BREND	They'll Know We Ar	PRH	36A
ST. BRIDE	Give To The Winds T	PH, UMH	21A, 35A
"	Out Of The Depths I	LCA, NCH, UMH	27A
ST. CATHERI	Faith Of Our Father	LCA, PH, PRH, UMH	23A, 32A, 65A
"	Faith Of The Martyr	NCH	32A, 65A, 67A
ST. CHRISTO	Before The Cross O	NCH, PH	19A
"	Beneath The Cross O	LCA, NCH, PH, PRH, UMH	19A, 27A
ST. COLUMBA	The King Of Love My	LCA, MSL, PH, PRH, UMH	64A
ST. DENIO	Immortal, Invisible	LCA, MSL, NCH, PH, PRH, UMH	12A, 35A, 62A
ST. DROSTAN	Ride On, Ride On In	LCA, MSL, NCH, PH	25A
ST. DUNSTAN	[All][He] Who Would	LCA, MSL, NCH, PH	09A, 47A, 60A
ST. GERTRUDE	Forward Through The	NCH, PH, UMH	36A, 51A
ST. HILDA	O Jesus, Thou Art St	LCA, PH	30A
ST. LOUIS	O Little Town Of Be	LCA, MSL, NCH, PH, PRH, UMH	04A, 05A
ST. MARGAR	O Love That [Will	LCA, NCH, PH, PRH, UMH	39A
ST. MICHAEL	O Day Of God, Draw	NCH, PH, UMH	16A, 63A
"	Send Down Thy Truth	PH	13A, 36A
ST. PETER	In Christ There Is	NCH, PH	14A 55A
"	Where Charity And L	NCH, UMH	14A
ST. PETERSB	I Sing The Praise Of	NCH	32A
"	Thou Hidden Source O	UMH	32A
ST. THEODUL	All Glory, Laud, And	LCA, MSL, NCH, PH, PRH, UMH	25A
"	O How Shall I Recei	NCH	02A
ST. THOMAS	I Love [Thy][Your]	NCH, PH, UMH	59A
"	Let Justice Flow Li	NCH	12A, 43A
SAFETY	Love Lifted Me	PRH, TSH	48A
SALZBURG	For The Brave Of Eve	PH	32A

SANDON	God Of Our Life, Th	NCH, PH	07A, 54A
"	Lead, Kindly Light	LCA, PH	62A
"	Unto The Hills We L	NCH	23A, 62A
SARUM	For All The Saints	LCA, MSL, PH, PRH, UMH	67A
SAXBY	Father In Heaven, W	PH	19A, 58A
SCARLET RI	Who Would Think Tha	NCH	06A
SCHÖNSTER	Beautiful [Jesus][Sa	LCA, MSL, NCH	30A
"	Fairest Lord Jesus	PH, PRH, UMH	30A
SCHUMANN	Your Ways Are Not O	NCH	09A, 52A
SEDONA	All Earth Is Waiting	GG	03A
SERENITY	Immortal Love, Fore	NCH, PH	40A, 49A
"	Serenity	UMH	40A, 49A
SERVANT SON	Won't You Let Me Be	NCH	52A
SICILIAN MA	Jesus, Friend, S	PH	43A
"	Lord, Dismiss Us W	LCA, MSL, NCH, PH, PRH, UMH	19A, 48A
SINE NOMINE	For All The Saint	LCA, MSL, NCH, PH, PRH, UMH	67A
SLANE	Be [Now][Thou] My	NCH, PH, PRH, UMH	09A, 35A, 61A
"	Lord Of All Hopeful	PH	09A, 38A
"	Take Time To Be Holy	PRH	58A
SOFTLY AND	Softly And Tenderly	LCA, NCH, PRH, UMH	55A, 59A
SOLID ROCK	My Hope Is Built On	NCH, UMH	66A
SONG 13	When My Love To God	PH	25A
SONG 24	I Greet Thee, Who	PH	62A
SONG 67	Within The Ma	PH	49A
SOUTHWELL	Have Faith In God,	PH, PRH	21A, 35A, 45A
SPARROW	God's Eye Is On The	NCH	42A, 46A
SPIRIT	Spirit, Spirit Of G	NCH	13A, 40A
SPLENDOR P	O Splendor Of God's	NCH, PH	01A
SPRING WOOD	Bless God, O My Soul	NCH	32A
"	Bless The Lord, O My	PRH	32A
STAND BY ME	Stand By Me	UMH	44A
STANLEY BE	We Meet You, O Chri	UMH	10A
STEADFAST	[O][Our] God, To Who	NCH, PH	59A
STILLE NACHT	Silent Night	LCA, MSL, NCH, PH, PRH, UMH	05A
STORIES O	Tell Me the [Story]	PRH, TSH, UMH	23A, 31A
STUTTGART	Come, [O][Thou] Lo	LCA, MSL, NCH, PH, UMH	01A, 02A
"	O My Soul, Bless	NCH, PH	57A
SUFFERER	He Never Said A Mu	UMH	27A
SURELY GO	Surely Goodness A	PRH	34A
SURSUM CORD	How Like A Gentle S	NCH, UMH	16A
SUTTON COM	Heal Me, Hands Of Je	UMH	40A
SWEETEST NA	There's Within My He	PRH, UMH	37A

228

W ZLOBIE LE	Christ Is [A]Risen!	UMH	28A
"	Infant Holy, Infant	PRH, UMH	05A
WACHET AUF	Keep Awake, Be Alwa	NCH	01A
"	Now Let Every Tongu	PH	08A
"	Wake, Awake, for Nig	LCA, MSL, NCH, PH, UMH	01A
WAHRES LICH	Dear [Master][Jesus]	PH	55A
WALSALL	O Lord And Master O	PH	33A, 61A
WAREHAM	O Splendor Of God's	UMH	01A
WAS GOTT T	God's Actions, Alwa	NCH	53A
"	Whate'er [My][Our]	LCA, PH	58A
WAS MEIN G	Who Trusts In God,	MSL, PH	40A, 49A, 63A
WE SHALL O	We Shall Overcome	NCH	20A, 44A, 66A
WEBB	Now Is The Time App	NCH	11A
"	Remember God Was	GG	11A, 47A
"	Stand Up, Stand Up	LCA, MSL, PH, PRH, UMH	11A
WEISSE FLAG	Alleluia! All	LCA, NCH	50A
"	Born Of God, Eternal	NCH	55A
"	Son Of God, Eternal	LCA, MSL, PH	55A
WELLESLEY	There's A Wideness	PH, UMH	15A, 41A
WELLINGTON	When Stephen, Full O	PH	32A
WELWYN	Children Of God	NCH	39A
"	O Brother Man, Fol	LCA, PH	39A, 59A
"	O God Of Strength	NCH	24A, 65A
"	O Holy God, Whose G	NCH	37A
WENTWORTH	My God, I Thank The	LCA, PH	68A
WER NUR D	If [You][Thou] But	LCA, MSL, NCH, PH, UMH	14A, 45A, 54A
WERE YOU T	Were You There	LCA, MSL, NCH, PH, PRH, UMH	19A, 27A, 28A
WIE SCHÖN	How Brightly Shines	PH	09A
"	O Morning Star, How	LCA, MSL, NCH, UMH	09A
WILTSHIRE	Through All The Cha	LCA, PH	38A
WINCHE NEW	Before Jehovah's Aw	LCA, MSL, PH	53A
"	The Baptist Shouts O	NCH	02A
WINCHE OLD	Behold Us, Lord A	LCA	20A, 35A
"	O Grant Us, God, A	NCH	20A, 35A
"	To Shepherds As They	MSL	02A
"	While Shepherds Watc	LCA, MSL, PH, PRH, UMH	02A
WIR PFLUGE	We [Plough][Plow]	LCA, PH	68A
WONDROUS L	What Wondrous Love	NCH, UMH	27A
WOODLANDS	Lift Up Your Heads	MSL	42A
"	Lift Up Your Heart	NCH, PH	42A
WOODWORTH	Just As I Am	LCA, MSL, NCH, PH, PRH, UMH	26A

WORDS OF L	Sing Them Over Agai	NCH, PRH, UMH	07A, 44A
WORLD PEAC	Let There Be Peace	UMH	30A, 49A
WRLD P PRA	Lead Us From Death	NCH	22A
WUNDERBARE	God Himself Is Wit	NCH, PH	29A, 59A

Y

YARNTON	We Are Not Our Own	NCH	14A, 48A
YORKSHIRE	Rejoice, O People,	PH	58A

Lectionary Preaching After Pentecost

The following index will aid the user of this book in matching the correct Sunday with the appropriate text during Pentecost. During the Pentecost season, this book lists Sundays by Proper (following the Revised Common and Episcopal lectionary system). Lutheran and Roman Catholic designations indicate days comparable to Sundays on which the Propers are used.

(Fixed dates do not pertain to Lutheran Lectionary)

Fixed Date Lectionaries *Revised Common (including ELCA)* *and Roman Catholic*	Lutheran Lectionary *Lutheran*
The Day of Pentecost	The Day of Pentecost
The Holy Trinity	The Holy Trinity
May 29-June 4 — Proper 4, Ordinary Time 9	Pentecost 2
June 5-11 — Proper 5, Ordinary Time 10	Pentecost 3
June 12-18 — Proper 6, Ordinary Time 11	Pentecost 4
June 19-25 — Proper 7, Ordinary Time 12	Pentecost 5
June 26-July 2 — Proper 8, Ordinary Time 13	Pentecost 6
July 3-9 — Proper 9, Ordinary Time 14	Pentecost 7
July 10-16 — Proper 10, Ordinary Time 15	Pentecost 8
July 17-23 — Proper 11, Ordinary Time 16	Pentecost 9
July 24-30 — Proper 12, Ordinary Time 17	Pentecost 10
July 31-Aug. 6 — Proper 13, Ordinary Time 18	Pentecost 11
Aug. 7-13 — Proper 14, Ordinary Time 19	Pentecost 12
Aug. 14-20 — Proper 15, Ordinary Time 20	Pentecost 13
Aug. 21-27 — Proper 16, Ordinary Time 21	Pentecost 14
Aug. 28-Sept. 3 — Proper 17, Ordinary Time 22	Pentecost 15
Sept. 4-10 — Proper 18, Ordinary Time 23	Pentecost 16
Sept. 11-17 — Proper 19, Ordinary Time 24	Pentecost 17
Sept. 18-24 — Proper 20, Ordinary Time 25	Pentecost 18
Sept. 25-Oct. 1 — Proper 21, Ordinary Time 26	Pentecost 19
Oct. 2-8 — Proper 22, Ordinary Time 27	Pentecost 20

Oct. 9-15 — Proper 23, Ordinary Time 28	Pentecost 21
Oct. 16-22 — Proper 24, Ordinary Time 29	Pentecost 22
Oct. 23-29 — Proper 25, Ordinary Time 30	Pentecost 23
Oct. 30-Nov. 5 — Proper 26, Ordinary Time 31	Pentecost 24
Nov. 6-12 — Proper 27, Ordinary Time 32	Pentecost 25
Nov. 13-19 — Proper 28, Ordinary Time 33	Pentecost 26
	Pentecost 27
Nov. 20-26 — Christ the King	Christ the King

Reformation Day (or last Sunday in October) is October 31 (Revised Common, Lutheran)

All Saints' Day (or first Sunday in November) is November 1 (Revised Common, Lutheran, Roman Catholic)